OSPREY COMBAT AIRCRAFT • 85

B-57 CANBERRA UNITS OF THE VIETNAM WAR

SERIES EDITOR: TONY HOLMES

OSPREY COMBAT AIRCRAFT • 85

B-57 CANBERRA UNITS OF THE VIETNAM WAR

T E BELL

OSPREY
PUBLISHING

Front Cover
On 15 March 1966, B-57Bs were sent into the Laotian Panhandle, not far from Tchepone and its famously deadly flak guns, to bomb troops and truck parks in the area. Among the crews to see action were Capt Larry Mason and his navigator Capt Jere Joyner of the 8th Bomb Squadron/6252nd Tactical Bomb Wing, flying B-57B 53-3906.

After dropping their bombs, Mason strafed an apparently disabled truck in the road. What he did not know was that this last target was a flak trap. The sky erupted with 57 mm rounds from at least six guns, the radar-directed flak tearing into the right wing and engine and a shell exploding in the rear cockpit. Then the right engine caught fire. Yet another round exploded in the cockpit, knocking out oxygen lines, instruments and communications. As Mason looked for suitable terrain over which to eject, Joyner passed forward a bloody note scrawled on the back of a reconnaissance photo. It read 'Hit badly arm and leg. Losing blood'.

Mason, fighting for control of the B-57, passed a tourniquet back to Joyner and, deciding his navigator could not survive an ejection, elected to fly the badly shot up Canberra back to Da Nang. The pilot, expecting to belly in, found to his relief that he was landing on three good wheels. In the end, Joyner had sustained 46 wounds from shell fragments and almost bled to death.

Capt Mason was awarded the Air Force Cross, the USAF's highest award for valour. Upon his recovery, Joyner received the Silver Star (*Cover Artwork by Gareth Hector*)

Title Page Spread Photograph
As the end neared for the B-57B in Southeast Asia, there were so few combat-worthy aircraft remaining, the two squadrons were combined into one – the 8th BS. The 13th BS went home to train for transition to the new B-57G, and it did not help when 16 aircraft were taken for conversion to that standard. Note that the tail codes of both units have been combined in this photo from Phan Rang in 1969. Soon, only the RAAF Canberra B 20s would remain at Phan Rang, one of which can just be seen in a revetment to the right of the B-57B (*Robert Mikesh Archive*)

First published in Great Britain in 2011 by Osprey Publishing
Midland House, West Way, Botley, Oxford, OX2 0PH
44-02 23rd St, Suite 219, Long Island City, New York, 11101

E-mail; info@ospreypublishing.com

ISBN: 978 1 84603 971 3
E-book ISBN: 978 1 84603 972 0

Edited by Tony Holmes
Page design by Tony Truscott
Cover Artwork by Gareth Hector
Aircraft Profiles by Jim Laurier
Index by Alan Thatcher
Originated by PDQ Digital Media Solutions, Suffolk, UK
Printed in China through Bookbuilders

11 12 13 14 15   10 9 8 7 6 5 4 3 2 1
Osprey Publishing is supporting the Woodland Trust, the UK's leading woodland conservation charity by funding the dedication of trees.

www.ospreypublishing.com

ACKNOWLEDGEMENTS
This book could not have come about without the help and encouragement of these people – Dr Robert P 'Bat' Bateman, USAF (Ret), Maj William 'Pappy' Boyington, USAF (Ret), Col Bob Butterfield, USAF (Ret), Sgt John M DeCillo, Joe English, Lt Col Richard Fontaine, USAF (Ret), Bob 'Godzilla' Galbreath, Bud Highleyman, Col Fleming Hobbs, USAF (Ret), Ross and Jan McMillan, Lt Col Larry Mason, USAF (Ret), Maj Gen William Maxson, USAF (Ret), Maj Robert Mikesh, USAF (Ret), Donald Nation, Col Nick Paldino, USAF (Ret), James Pickles, Maj Ed Rider, USAF (Ret), Maj George B Rose, USAF (Ret), Col Joseph M Rup Jr, USAF (Ret), Lt Col Mike Thorn, USAF (Ret), Lt Col Robert L Wilkerson, USAF (Ret), Terry Zimmer and Andrew Thomas.

CONTENTS

HOT WAR, COLD BEGINNING

It can hardly be understated just how close the B-57B Canberra, which Martin developed from the classic do-everything British design, came to being one of those fine, journeyman aircraft that served its time in the inventory before becoming virtually forgotten. It might have ended up like so many others that came and went in the Cold War without much fanfare and, more significantly, ignominiously retired with a spotty operational record and having never fired a shot in anger.

The prime example of an aircraft in this category would be the Boeing B-47 Stratojet. Considered by many to be a milestone aircraft in the history of flight, almost 2000 examples of this first-generation, six-engined jet bomber were built – a figure unheard of for a peacetime bomber before or since, and one which is never likely to be matched. We now live in an age where tactical and strategic aircraft types are built in relatively tiny numbers, are prohibitively expensive and are decades in the making. However, modern military aircraft are expected to stay in the inventory for no less than 30 or 40 years, or even longer.

The B-47 bomber force stayed in the USAF inventory for less than 15 years after first deployment, with the whole fleet going from drawing board to smelter in less than 20 years. The V-22 Osprey took that long to go from concept to operational status! Of course, it must be pointed out that the Stratojet was never thought of as anything other than a first-strike nuclear bomber. Although it was quite capable of carrying conventional weapons, it never did so operationally, and crews were scarcely trained in their use. So it was not a terribly flexible airframe, despite successful electronic countermeasures (ECM) and reconnaissance versions being built in small numbers. But what has this to do with the B-47's contemporary, the US version of the English Electric Canberra?

Before historical events intervened, the B-57B, too, was on its way to the same Arizona desert boneyard that was home to rows and rows of mouldering B-47s awaiting the scrapper. In fact many ex-Stratojet pilots and navigators were retrained to fly the B-57 in the late 1950s.

By the early 1960s, RB-57As and early-production B-57Bs had already been relegated to the Air National Guard (ANG) and other non-frontline users. Compared to the B-47, it had been built in such small numbers, and was no longer at the cutting edge of military aviation technology – certainly not when compared to its other, much larger contemporary, the B-52 – that the jet would have become, in its light-bomber/intruder configuration, little more than a minor Cold War footnote. The high-altitude, 'long-wing' versions, the RB-57D and R/WB-57F models, were highly successful reconnaissance platforms, but they were in a class of their own, having little in common with the intruder marks.

Below and Right
The patches worn by personnel of the 8th and 13th BSs. Both were among the oldest units in the USAF, tracing their lineage back to the US Army Air Service in World War 1. They had been active ever since, and had fought in every US conflict. The 13th was famous for its B-26 Invader night interdiction exploits during the Korean War. The 13th's skeletal mascot is known as 'Oscar' to this day, with the squadron presently flying the Northrop B-2 Spirit stealth bomber

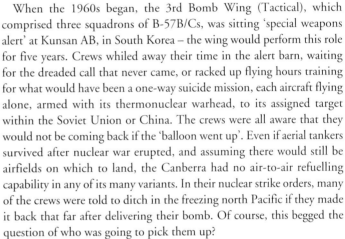

This rare photograph from the late-1950s shows an early 3rd BW B-57C 53-3856, which was one of only 38 dual-control versions of the B-57B built. The aircraft, wearing the then-standard scheme of overall gloss black, appears to be on a ferry flight, probably stopped over in Alaska on its way to or from Yokota AB, Japan. Note the F-84Fs and T-33As in the background with their high-visibility arctic markings. 53-3856 served with the 8th BS at Clark AFB prior to being transferred back to Florida in 1968 to help train crews to fly the new B-57G as part of Project *Harvest Moon* (*via James Pickles*)

When the 1960s began, the 3rd Bomb Wing (Tactical), which comprised three squadrons of B-57B/Cs, was sitting 'special weapons alert' at Kunsan AB, in South Korea – the wing would perform this role for five years. Crews whiled away their time in the alert barn, waiting for the dreaded call that never came, or racked up flying hours training for what would have been a one-way suicide mission, each aircraft flying alone, armed with its thermonuclear warhead, to its assigned target within the Soviet Union or China. The crews were all aware that they would not be coming back if the 'balloon went up'. Even if aerial tankers survived after nuclear war erupted, and assuming there would still be airfields on which to land, the Canberra had no air-to-air refuelling capability in any of its many variants. In their nuclear strike orders, many of the crews were told to ditch in the freezing north Pacific if they made it back that far after delivering their bomb. Of course, this begged the question of who was going to pick them up?

So by 1964 the 8th, 13th and 90th Bomb Squadrons and their parent 3rd BW, which was part of the Pacific Air Forces (PACAF), had settled into a somewhat monotonous routine of sitting alert and training, training and more sitting alert. The USAF's plan for the wing was oblivion. After all, the B-57B was considered an interim aircraft from the outset, built to meet an immediate need that planners considered filled now by new, modern types like the F-105 Thunderchief, which was finally up and running and deployed all over the world. The three Canberra squadrons within the 3rd BW were to return to the US and hand their aircraft over to ANG units. Indeed, some jets had already been sent home when events changed the B-57's lot dramatically.

Meanwhile, in a Southeast Asian country very few Americans could even locate on a map, the US government was already deeply involved in a proxy fight supporting one side in a long-running civil war that had already drained the French and sent them home in disgrace. After the communist Viet Minh defeated French forces in 1954, both sides signed the Geneva Accords, which returned the former colony to the native population and called for no more external interference in Vietnamese affairs. To mollify the anti-communist south, the country was partitioned along the 17th Parallel. The North Vietnamese, however, had no intention of leaving their country split in two and, under the leadership of Ho Chi Minh, were determined to impose their political system on the entire nation, while kicking any remaining meddling foreigners out.

While only the most cynical US politicians and generals could call South Vietnam a 'democracy', at least in the minds of the 'politicos' they were not communists. The North Vietnamese were, and it was no secret that they were being supplied by the Soviets and the communist Chinese with everything from rice to heavy artillery pieces and jet fighters.

To achieve their ends in the South, an indigenous guerrilla army, derisively called the Viet Cong (VC), was raised through a combination of impressment and the recruiting of idealistic young men and women. Local villages and farmers were taxed in the form of rice and other commodities, and penalties were harsh for those who did not pay their tribute to the VC. In order to supply this army of irregulars, the North created and maintained a vast and ingenious network of roads, jungle trails, truck parks, maintenance facilities, fuel dumps, barracks, underground hospitals, ammunition dumps, roadwork machinery and repair crews, plus anti-aircraft artillery (AAA) units to protect it all.

This was the famous Ho Chi Minh Trail, which began in North Vietnam and ran for hundreds of miles just inside and parallel to the Laotian border. Marked by countless detours and arteries, the road and trail system made its way the entire length of South Vietnam. It is here in Laos, where the 'Secret War' was fought, that much of the B-57's story takes place. As hard as it is to imagine now, during their eight years flying and fighting from bases in South Vietnam and Thailand, the majority of the jet's war was classified. It was conducted under the usual testosterone-soaked codenames favoured by US military men – *Barrel Roll, Steel Tiger* and *Tiger Hound* were three that involved the Canberra. These names referred to areas of Laos being bombed by American aircraft, with *Barrel Roll* denoting missions in the north, and *Steel Tiger* and *Tiger Hound* missions in the southern and northern areas of the panhandle.

While the US denied it was conducting operations in Laos, so the Vietnamese lied about their supply line that ran almost the entire length of that unfortunate land, and they denied that they had as many as 45,000 troops in Laos to defend the Ho Chi Minh Trail. So, true to the paradoxes that attach to the actions of nations, the only people from whom this war was a secret were the populations of the countries who were pulling the strings that kept the war going – the Soviet Union, China and the US. Australia, which also had troops and aircraft in the war, similarly kept the truth about this secret war from its own people.

ON TENTERHOOKS

On 2 April 1964, plans to send the B-57B/C units home were officially changed, and a week later the first 12 jets from the 13th BS were sent from their permanent home of Yokota AB, Japan, to Clark AFB in the Philippines, followed eight days later by the first of the 8th BS's Canberras. By month-end all 47 of the two squadrons' machines were in place at Clark, having been assigned to the F-100D-equipped 405th Fighter Wing (FW). The 3rd BW's other unit, the 90th BS, had already detached from the wing and moved to England, AFB, Louisiana, for transition to the F-100D fighter-bomber. So the 'Yellowbirds' (8th BS) and the 'Redbirds' (13th BS) were all that remained of the former wing.

Throughout that first summer after the 8th and 13th had been deployed to the Philippines, tension rose and fell on base among rumours of an impending deployment to a shooting war in Vietnam. Indeed, USAF reconnaissance and interceptor units had already been transferred to Tan Son Nhut airport in Saigon. Toward the end of July, the rumours surrounding the B-57s' commitment to the escalating conflict had reached fever pitch, and they were not without foundation.

President Lyndon Johnson's administration was champing at the bit for any excuse to introduce jet bombers into Vietnam, but it had been held back so far in observance of the Geneva Accords (even though the US had refused to sign it). This document was, however, being violated with impunity – particularly in Laos – by both sides, but it was hard to hide squadrons of jet bombers and fighter-bombers in South Vietnam.

The Vietnamese Air Force (VNAF) was a largely ineffective outfit whose offensive capability was made up primarily of A-1E/H Skyraiders and armed T-28 Trojan trainers. South Vietnamese, Laotian and US pilots had been flying the Trojans covertly on strikes just inside the North Vietnamese borders, further provoking the communists.

During this time, a few B-57B crews got an early introduction to Vietnam. They acted as secret couriers, flying their Canberras from base to base between Clark and Thailand and among various airfields in South Vietnam. These crews shuttled copies of orders, reconnaissance photos and other sensitive documents between the various HQs and, according to some who flew these missions, they also delivered such essential war-fighting equipment as steaks and lobsters for general officers! One who flew the courier route was navigator 1Lt Fleming Hobbs;

'In April 1964 four aircraft deployed to Tan Son Nhut and flew courier missions carrying classified documents to bases throughout the area. We would fly to Bangkok and to two other bases in Thailand, stopping at Udorn AB, also in Thailand, for breakfast at the CIA-run Air America club. Then we'd go on to Da Nang before heading back to Tan Son Nhut. At the bases, other than Udorn for refuelling and breakfast, we just stopped at the end on the runway, kept the engines running, had someone sign for the material and took off again.'

For most B-57 crews however, Vietnam remained a mystery. All they knew was that it was a war in the making, and that they would be at the tip of the spear when politicians decided to poke it at the communists.

At last, the US administration got the excuse it needed to move in a big way against the North. The US Navy had made itself a sizeable presence in the waters off Vietnam for some time, but had not yet engaged the North Vietnamese. This all changed on the evening of 2 August 1964. Under the command of Rear Admiral George Stephen Morrison (the father of Jim Morrison, leader of *The Doors*), the US fleet in the Tonkin Gulf was seen by the North Vietnamese as part of an overall scheme of provocation against them. And although their hands were not clean either, US intelligence history, since declassified, bears this out.

USS *Maddox* (DD-731), a signal intelligence-tasked destroyer that was part of operations codenamed *Desoto*, was attacked by three North Vietnamese Navy torpedo boats of the 135th Torpedo Squadron. The *Maddox* returned fire, expending almost 300 three- and five-inch shells. Also, US Navy F-8 Crusader fighters launched from the aircraft carrier

USS *Ticonderoga* (CVA-14) strafed the patrol boats with 20 mm rounds. One of the F-8s was damaged, and a single 14.5 mm round hit the *Maddox*. All three North Vietnamese torpedo boats were damaged and four communist sailors were reported killed, with six more wounded.

The following night, the destroyer USS *Turner Joy* (DD-951) was also allegedly attacked by North Vietnamese naval craft. However, history has since shown that the second attack almost certainly never occurred, and while the *Turner Joy* unleashed a number of rounds, the firing has been ascribed to a tense and overexcited crew working in bad weather, heaving seas and at night, with only radar and sonar with which to see. It would not be until 2005 that official documents were declassified showing that those who did not believe the *Turner Joy* had been attacked were right all along (among the doubters was future Medal of Honor recipient Cdr James Stockdale, one of the Crusader pilots launched on the night of 4 August), and that the US government was aware of this at the time. It would be one of the first times – though far from the last – that major errors of fact and distortion of the truth on both sides would influence the conduct of the war in Vietnam.

Following these clashes the Johnson administration now had the 'incident' it wanted, and facts were not going to get in the way. The President took his case to Congress, which passed the so-called Tonkin Gulf Resolution. This granted Johnson virtual carte blanche to wage war – ostensibly in assistance of any Southeast Asian nation considered by the administration to be threatened by 'communist aggression'. Besides allowing Johnson to deploy all the tactical jets he wanted into the theatre, he was also given the go-ahead to send ground troops at his discretion, all without the usual need for a declaration of war. So in the unusual language of politicians of the day, particularly in the Johnson cabinet, Vietnam was never a 'war', but rather 'assistance'. It was not even given the dignity of the term 'police action', which was the phrase used officially to describe the war in Korea little more than ten years earlier.

What this meant for the B-57 squadrons was orders to get ready to go to Vietnam. Clark AFB was already on a wartime footing, and over the next 48 hours orders to deploy either to Thailand or to Bien Hoa AB, near Saigon, were sent down, only to be withdrawn at the last minute. The stress on the crews, and their families who lived with them at Clark, was enormous. But these orders, and then orders rescinding them, continued. Finally, after both squadrons had been stood down for the night, the real thing was ordered. It turned out to be a disaster, one of the first of several to befall the squadrons in the coming year. Indeed, during those early months in combat there would be whispers that the two squadrons were 'bad luck' units, a wholly undeserved reputation that would be well and truly put down soon enough. Still, every man, air- or groundcrew, in the 'Yellowbirds' and the 'Redbirds' would have their nerve, character and courage severely tested during this time, and men would die in ways that could never have been anticipated.

Just before midnight on 4 August, following the *Turner Joy* 'incident' and 36 unbearable hours of being called to war and then sent home, the long-awaited orders came to go to Vietnam. Then, just after dawn, the crews were once again stood down, told to go home and await further orders. Finally, that evening, the real thing came down and

The 8th BS flightline at Bien Hoa remained a crowded place in the spring of 1965 as the rainy season began. Note that the aircraft still bear their plane-in-squadron identifying letters. Many of these jets are replacements flown in from US ANG units for those destroyed in the 1 November 1964 mortar attack. Very soon a number of these aircraft would be lost in an even greater tragic event (*Robert Galbreath*)

During the ill-fated deployment from Clark AFB in the Philippines to Bien Hoa on the night of 5-6 August, 1964, 53-3884 of the 13th BS was involved in a runway collision with 53-3877 while landing in bad weather at Bien Hoa. The collision, followed by another aircraft blowing a tyre upon landing, caused the runway to be closed and all following flights to be diverted to Tan Son Nhut. In the event, this aircraft was damaged enough to be written off (*Robert Galbreath*)

the two squadrons were ordered to send 20 aircraft to Bien Hoa 'as soon as possible'. According to historian and Vietnam combat pilot Robert Mikesh's definitive history of the B-57, 'Crews had already been assigned to aircraft, and now flight plans to this just announced destination were hastily prepared for the five flights of four aircraft each. Lt Col Billy McLeod, commander of the 13th BS, led the first flight off at 1900 hrs, and each succeeding flight launched at 20-30 minute intervals'.

There was one huge problem looming. B-57 crews had been trained to fly their missions alone, carrying nuclear weapons. They were not trained for night formation flying and, in this case, flying over water the entire route without modern navigational aids to a destination few of them had ever been to. While the flights got off without incident, the worst lay ahead for them, and in the circumstances, what happened was inevitable.

It was the summer monsoon season, and when the jets began arriving at Bien Hoa in the darkness, the ceiling was down to 700 ft during a heavy rain squall. According to Mikesh, 'Uncertainties after landing caused one aircraft to delay on the runway, allowing another with loss of hydraulic brake pressure to overtake it in the darkness and collide with it. As a result 53-3884 was a write-off'. The other aircraft, 53-3877, was put back in the air only after considerable repairs were made. The runway was completely fouled after another aircraft blew both tyres on its landing roll out. So far, miraculously, none of the crews had been injured.

With the Bien Hoa active runway shut down, the remainder of the aircraft were diverted to busy Tan Son Nhut, some 12 miles away.

It was then that tragedy intervened. Capt Fred Cutrer and his navigator 1Lt Leonard Lee Kaster were killed when their aircraft (53-3870) crashed into the Song Dong Nai River 25 miles northeast of Bien Hoa. The reasons for the crash were never established, and theories have ranged from enemy fire to the pilot flying into the ground while on a TACAN (Tactical Air Navigation) approach in bad weather. Because the crash occurred in VC-controlled territory, it took weeks for the bodies of the crew to be recovered.

The Bien Hoa B-57s now were under the operational control of the 2nd Air Division (AD), commanded by Gen Joseph Moore. The 2nd AD reported to Gen William C Westmoreland, Commander, Military Assistance Command, Vietnam.

On 9 August, the first Sunday after the arrival of the two squadrons, Air Commodore Nguyen Cao Ky (who would become prime minister in 1965 as head of the country's military junta in one of South Vietnam's typically turbulent power shifts), spoke at the Bien Hoa Officers' Club welcoming the B-57 crews. He told the assembled Americans that his country had enjoyed no peace since Vietnam was partitioned in 1954 – in fact, Vietnam had seen no peace since long before World War 2. Ky did not mince his words, stating that 'Night after night, day in and day out, there is no time while one cannot witness shelled hamlets, scorched homes and crying survivors looking helplessly for their disembowelled babies, their beheaded wives or their mutilated beloved ones'.

The two squadrons were, for the time being, mixed together at Bien Hoa, and this included their maintenance and support operations as well. The combined units formally came under the control of the 405th Air Division (ADVON) 1. Maintenance facilities at Bien Hoa were scarce, and this meant that the B-57s had to share an open-air, three-sided hangar with VNAF A-1 Skyraiders. In early January 1965, three U-2s arrived at Bien Hoa, so they were immediately given maintenance and runway priority over the B-57s and A-1Es. The U-2s rotated back and forth to Kadena AB, Okinawa, or Hill AFB, Utah.

When the B-57s, their crews and maintenance personnel were finally in place at Bien Hoa, so began six long months of them playing the role of political pawns. The US government had no intention of using the bombers yet, so their sole purpose in-theatre was to show off American muscle. However, as serviceable jets became more scarce, aircrews were unable to show the locals much of anything. The 405th ADVON 1 crews did get to fly a few unarmed 'reconnaissance' missions, but these were barely frequent enough to allow them to stay current on the B-57. 'We would fly a half-hour hop, then leave the jet running so another crew could strap in and fly for another half-hour or so. It was ridiculous', recalled a pilot at Bien Hoa at the time. Morale plummeted.

While security was always on the minds of the Americans at Bien Hoa, in those early months of the deployment it remained nothing more than a subject of conversation. Since the base was a VNAF installation, guarding the airfield from attack was the responsibility of South Vietnamese forces, whose attitude toward that task, to put it kindly, was somewhat relaxed. US air- and groundcrews rightly saw their aircraft (and themselves) as sitting ducks for a VC attack, with the valuable B-57s parked cheek-by-jowl on the open tarmac every night, bombs stacked nearby, making for fat targets. As Robert Mikesh put it, 'Everyone talked of these possibilities, but no one did anything about it'.

As on bases all over South Vietnam, by day the locals worked as maids, janitors, labourers and in other menial jobs. By night, many of them were VC soldiers and spies, or were otherwise sympathetic to the communist cause (although this by no means applied to all of the indigenous workers). So the VC had no problem obtaining detailed maps of US installations like Bien Hoa. And very soon the US brass would come to rue their casual attitude toward base security.

31 October 1964 was yet another day of flying seemingly endless unarmed road-reconnaissance missions which, while familiarising the aircrews with the lay of the land, were viewed as little more than make-work. By dusk on this Halloween, the aircraft had been parked for the night on the Bien Hoa ramp. As usual, the B-57s sat

out in the open in four rows of five aircraft, parked wing to wing. There were no revetments or hardened aircraft shelters on the base. With no warning, at 0025 hrs on 1 November, 81 mm mortar rounds began dropping into the American side of the base, exploding in the B-57 parking area. Later, investigators were able to determine that only six mortars, placed about a quarter-of-a-mile outside the perimeter, were needed to do the job. The mortars had been perfectly registered and the gun crews had managed to land as many as 80 rounds inside the base before disappearing into the night. It was all over within minutes.

All around aircraft and buildings burned, the fires lighting up the damage to the base and its precious aircraft. However, the dawn would bring the full reality of their vulnerability into focus for the base's occupants. It was clear that the aircraft parking area and the US compound near the centre of the base were the primary targets.

Even though the B-57s were not flying combat missions at the time, many jets were kept 'bombed up' and loaded with 20 mm ammunition, ready for combat. When the mortar rounds began to fall, the tarmac was littered with 500-lb bombs. Groundcrew spent most of the night hastily removing the bombs from the parking ramp and stacking them away from the fires. The bombs could have begun to 'cook off' at any moment, but in large part due to the fast work of the armourers and other groundcrew none did. Armourer Terry Zimmer recalled;

'After working our usual long day our crew went to the airmens' club, and on the way back to our hut I remember saying how quiet it was. Nights at Bien Hoa were usually like the 4th of July. In the distance you could see tracer rounds, an occasional bomb going off and flares being dropped, lighting up the night sky. The silence changed at midnight. Mortars started going off and it seemed like fire was everywhere. I think everyone set a record getting dressed and making our way to the

flightline, where the real damage was. Aeroplanes were on fire and ammo was going off. Our job was to get the bombs off the jets before they could cause more damage.

'As I think back about that night there was one thing missing, and that was any sign of fear. They say adrenalin is the body's morphine, and whoever coined that phrase hit

Just after midnight on 1 November 1964, the VC hit the USAF flightline at Bien Hoa with a mortar barrage, destroying five Canberras outright and damaging the remaining 15, whilst also destroying the base's HH-43 rescue helicopter and two C-47s. Here, with the remains of one B-57 in the foreground, 53-3924 shows that its wing tank exploded, burning a large portion of the wing. This aircraft was subsequently written off. Crowded conditions at the base created an easy target for the VC (*Terry Zimmer*)

An unidentified B-57 burned down to its engine compressors by the tremendous heat of the fires started by the 81 mm mortar rounds that fell into the USAF flightline at Bien Hoa at 0025 hrs on 1 November 1964. In addition to the US aircraft losses, the VNAF had three A-1H Skyraiders destroyed and three damaged. Four Americans were killed and 72 others wounded. Base defence, which was the responsibility of the South Vietnamese, was considered poor. It was subsequently taken up by Australian troops (*Terry Zimmer*)

Another victim of the Bien Hoa attack was 52-1555 of the 8th BS. This was one of the early B-57B aircraft armed with eight 0.50-cal machine guns. The guns can be discerned from the burnt-out wing by their perforated cooling jackets, which are exposed in this photograph. The aircraft was a complete write-off and was scavenged for parts. The five B-57s lost in the attack were immediately replaced by aircraft taken from stateside ANG units equipped with the type (*Terry Zimmer*)

Fuselage speed brakes out, wing 'fingers' deployed and arming wires trailing from empty pylons, B-57B 53-3929 returns to Bien Hoa after one of the early armed missions flown by the 8th BS just before what would become known as the 'Bien Hoa Holocaust'. This aircraft was later converted into a B-57G and survived the war

the nail on the head. Everyone took care of business.'

When daylight arrived, it was learnt that four Americans had been killed and another 72 wounded in the attack. Five of the 20 B-57B/C aircraft had been destroyed and of those, two had been burned to the point that only their engines remained relatively intact. Not one Canberra had escaped some degree of damage. Four VNAF A-1Hs were also destroyed in the shelling.

The Americans had lost a quarter of their in-country aircraft without having yet fired a single shot in anger. The B-57B and dual-control C-model had not been built in great numbers, and of those, only the later blocks remained in frontline service, so losses like these were not easily absorbed. Attrition and the attendant aircraft shortages would haunt the two combat squadrons all the way to the bitter end.

B-57 pilot Capt Pete Hall was on the base when it got mortared that night. He recalled;

'They replaced our aeroplanes immediately. They took them from the Kentucky ANG and we flew them in their markings for a while. I don't know how they got us those replacement aeroplanes so fast. One thing about those jets – they had four 0.50-cal guns in each wing instead of the standard four 20 mm guns we had (two in each wing, bore-sighted for strafing. Those little 0.50-cal guns weren't any good.'

Later, still more of the older B-57s were brought in from the Nevada and Kentucky ANGs. 'Redbird' and 'Yellowbird' crews would have to get used to them though, for as attrition took a greater toll on the Canberra force in South Vietnam more of the early B-models would be cherry-picked from ANG units in the US. All B-57Bs with serial numbers prior to 52-1576 boasted the eight 0.50-cal guns, and their fitment took away the punch of the HEI (High-Explosive Incendiary) rounds fired by the quartet of M-39 20 mm cannon.

More of the older ANG Canberras would be appropriated before the war was all over. Indeed, attrition was to become so bad that eventually the two units would have to be combined to make a single squadron.

AT LONG LAST, FLYING IN ANGER

On 19 February 1965, with crews of the 8th and 13th BSs wondering just what they were doing in a combat zone without being allowed to join the fight, everything changed. For weeks rumours had been circulating at Bien Hoa that the squadrons would be going out on a combat mission any day now. That day finally arrived on 19 February, when two flights of four aircraft each took off and, along with a handful of F-100D Super Sabres, pounded VC targets near Bien Gia, in Puoc Tuy Province, some 40 miles east of Saigon.

While many of these early sorties were flown with as many as 20 B-57s airborne at once, tactics were soon changed and the Canberras flew their missions in ones and twos. However, while they participated in the Operation *Rolling Thunder* bombing campaign the big flights did their job. Indeed, in a mission against the Man Yang pass on Route 19 on 21 February, bombs from B-57s and F-100s were credited with saving a company of 220 soldiers from the Army of the Republic of Vietnam (ARVN), and their US advisers, who were surrounded by the VC.

On 11 March the 'Yellowbirds' lost their first crew on a *Rolling Thunder* bombing strike. Pilot Capt William Carroll Mattis and his navigator 1Lt Richard Dean Smith perished when their B-57B (53-3890) was seen by their wingman to suddenly burst into flames and explode while bombing a target 30 miles northeast of Kontum. It is believed that the jet was destroyed by the explosions from its own 500-lb bombs, which were released from low altitude. Mattis' body was recovered shortly after the crash, but Smith's remains were not found until 1994.

Pilot Bob Butterfield arrived at Clark AFB in 1965 and began flying combat missions almost immediately. Butterfield had flown just about every tactical aircraft in the inventory by this time, and had decided he preferred the ground attack role, and specifically the B-57B. In those early days most of the combat missions were flown in daylight;

'The B-57 was originally needed for the air-to-ground role in the Korean War. We didn't have a fast strike aircraft with a good bomb load to get in and out of the target area, and the AAA batteries were taking a toll on our main air-to-ground aircraft, the B-26 Invader, also flown by the 13th BS. The decision was made to produce the British Canberra – a light, low-level,

B-57B 53-3888 is shown here becoming the first American jet bomber to drop ordnance in combat. The aircraft was loaded with two M117 750-lb bombs under each wing and nine 500-lb 'box-fin' general purpose bombs, and it expended them on 19 February 1965 in an attack on a VC position in a field near Bien Gia, just east of Saigon, and not far from the aircraft's base at Bien Hoa. Its crew consisted of pilot, Maj Howard F O'Neal, commander of the 13th BS, and his navigator, Maj Frank R Chandler. They were dropping on a target marked by a FAC's smoke rocket (*USAF*)

twin-engined jet bomber, and to modify it for the dive-bombing and strafing roles.

'Martin stressed the wings for dive-bombing and added four 20 mm cannon (with a total of 1060 rounds of ammunition) or eight 0.50-cal machine guns in the wings. The rotary bomb-bay could hold up to 4500 lbs of ordnance, with an additional 4000-lb capacity under the wings. The fuel tanks would permit up to four hours of flying time for the 55,000-lb aircraft with ordnance. These characteristics made this aeroplane the best close air support (CAS) weapon in the Vietnam War.

'From the crew members' perspective, the 440-knot maximum speed was not fast enough in some "hot" areas, and the big wings offered a large target for the gunners. However, the late 1940s technology of a non-hydraulic flight control system (made up of torque tubes and blow-back rods) made the aeroplane harder to knock down than most jets at that time that had a standard hydraulic flight control system. For example, I took a hit through the elevator control rod on one mission and kept flying because I didn't have any indications of a problem. When I landed the crew chief pointed out the holes in the back of the fuselage. The rod took the hit, but it didn't affect the control of the aircraft.'

For missions flown with forward air controllers (FACs) in O-1 Bird Dogs, the B-57s usually flew in four-aircraft flights, and during the first months of combat in 1965 they flew day missions. Since one Canberra could, and usually did, carry nine 500-lb bombs internally, four 750-lb bombs under the wings and 1060 rounds of 20 mm ammunition, when this was multiplied by four the sheer amount of firepower at the FAC's disposal frequently overwhelmed him. He usually only had one target planned per flight of A-1 Skyraiders or F-100 Super Sabres.

Pilot 1Lt Fleming Hobbs recalled what it was like working with a FAC when flying a heavily armed Canberra;

'After we smashed target one, we usually followed the FAC to another target and then another after that. We had the bombs, we had the fuel and we had the accuracy they liked. Other missions besides those directed by FACs were road interdiction strikes in southern and northern Laos. The latter sorties saw us operating primarily over Routes 6 and 65 (in the Operation *Barrel Roll* area). Those were almost four-hour missions, and it was 650 nautical miles up there. We went in two flights of four, five minutes apart, or four flights of four, five minutes apart. Yes, that's 16 B-57s on a road segment or road intersection with a total 208 bombs. Outbound started at 29,000 ft at 390 knots true airspeed at altitude (KTAS), and then we'd descend into the target area, spot the target, make two to three passes – not more due to being short of fuel at that long range – and climb back for home. Return was at plus or minus 50,000 ft/390 KTAS, and an amazingly low fuel flow of 2200 lbs per hour.'

However, on these missions all this firepower was occasionally wasted partly due to the no-frills nature of the B-57, as Hobbs explained;

'We had no good navigation equipment – we used TACAN and eyeballs. Later, Pakistani B-57s actually got a radar – what a luxury! And the TACANs didn't cover those areas way up north. If we had targets at shorter range, we could have dropped down to low level and visually navigated to the exact spot, but at 650 nautical miles, fuel limitations made that out of the question.

'The descent was from 30,000 ft to around 9000 ft ASL (Above Sea Level) – 4000 ft terrain elevation plus our dive bomb roll-in height of 5000 ft. This took five to five-and-a-half minutes, and we travelled about 33 nautical miles in that time. So it was fairly accurate, and if the roads didn't look exactly as briefed we didn't have time to "scout" the area at lower altitude for the exact spot. However, all roads up there were travelled only by the North Vietnamese, and any road was a target. We used our four 750-lb bombs first, dropped hot, and the nine 500 "pounders" were dropped later and armed with six-, 12- and 24-hour delayed fuses. They would bury themselves in the dirt and explode later.'

Fusing the bombs to explode at different times made life especially treacherous for the North Vietnamese Army (NVA) and VC repair gangs. However, as shall be seen, the time-delay fuses could just as easily turn upon their masters with devastating effect.

'Now navigation equipment, or lack thereof, was problem one, and problem two was the weather', continued Hobbs. 'In the spring the Laotians would burn land to accomplish slash-and-burn agriculture. The smoke and haze would fill the air. When you descended to 9000 ft to roll-in on the target, which was supposed to be about one to two miles to your left, often you could barely see the ground in the haze. If there was no road in sight we would make a slow turn and find the target or any road we could see'.

When it came to ordnance, even before the wizardry of the B-57G came on the scene, the B-models could, and did, carry just about any kind of bomb or rocket in the USAF inventory. However, after early experimentation, the B-57 squadrons arrived at the most effective weapons for their particular aeroplane and missions.

Most commonly, especially in the early stages of the war, the B-57Bs mounted 750-lb bombs on the four wing pylons. They could also carry 21 250-lb fragmentation bombs or, more commonly, nine 500-lb general purpose bombs in the rotary bay. Both the latter feature and the wing hardpoints were unique to the Canberra in US military service. The bomb-bay door was pivoted longitudinally along its centreline, and the bombs were shackled directly to the inside of the door. Just prior to release, an electric motor rolled the door over and exposed the bombs to the slipstream. After the bombs were dropped, the door rotated shut, leaving the jet aerodynamically clean once again.

Pilot Capt Pete Hall recalled;

'At the time, our primary mission was nuclear, but when Vietnam started we were sent down to Clark AFB, where we had a bombing range of our own known as "Crow Valley". There, we did our training with conventional weapons. Our bombing range was quite close to the base. We would take off in a

In those heady early days of combat for the Canberra crews, flak damage was still a novel thing. Here, a group of airmen examine a shrapnel hole near the cockpit of this B-57B after it took flak hits whilst attacking the Xom Bang ammunition depot on 2 March 1965. Capt George Rose, third from left, was the pilot on that mission (*via George Rose*)

Sgt E Brusseau, an armourer at Bien Hoa, de-arms the 0.50-cal machine guns following a combat mission by 8th BS B-57B 52-1545. This jet was one of the early-production models taken from the Kansas ANG to replace aircraft lost in the mortar attack on the base. It survived the war and finished its career with the Vermont ANG (*via John DeCillo*)

The B-57's unique bomb-bay and door system was quite versatile and could carry a variety of weapons, which were attached directly to the rotating one-piece door. This jet has been loaded with 27 100-lb general purpose bombs, in this case World War 2 relics that were rarely used in Vietnam. Small bombs like these were loaded two deep, allowing more to be carried internally and leaving the underwing pylons free for other weapons (*John DeCillo*)

four-ship in trail, 15 seconds apart, and by the time we had changed to the range radio frequency we were already in the pattern for the range.

'We could carry 21 250-lb fragmentation bombs internally, along with four Napalm bombs or four seven-shot rocket pods externally. In combat, we found the 2.75-in folding-fin aerial rockets (FFARs) to be inaccurate. They were also old and unreliable. They would send us out over Laos at night with these things, and one might have a fin that didn't open, sending the rocket off all crazy. Occasionally, they would go off inside the pod. They were left over from Korea or World War 2. Finally, when we got down to the last six or eight pods, I told my squadron commander that I was going out over the water to fire those things off so we wouldn't have to use them in combat anymore. One of them went wild and almost killed my wingman.'

1Lt Fleming Hobbs had even more contempt for the rockets. 'We even carried eight wing stations of nine-tube rocket pods each once. Those 2.75-in rockets with a 1.5-lb warhead were useless. Every time I see Hueys firing those I think of how much better throwing rocks would be.

'There was a bomb shortage for a time in 1965-66. Faster aircraft could not carry many bombs, while we and the A-1s could. That's how we ended up carrying M35 and M36 incendiary cluster bombs. Hell, if they had run out of them we might have ended up dropping empty leaflet bombs! Since we did not drop at over 400 knots, we were certified to carry 500-lb box fin bombs from World War 2. Nine of these would fit well in the bomb-bay. Four M117s (750-lb bombs with modern, aerodynamic fin units) on the wing were preferred, but the 500-lb box fins were okay, as was one 1000-lb box fin on each wing.'

The M35/36 incendiary cluster unit was in a class all by itself. It was a devastating and terrifying weapon that was used almost exclusively by the B-57s. No other tactical air branch was interested in these large, unwieldy weapons, and so they were used first by the early, clandestine B-26 Invader crews who flew interdiction missions on the 'Trail', and they duly passed them down to the B-57 units. These munitions were perfect for truck parks, convoys, troops bivouacked in the open, ammunition and rice dumps and, in fact, anything else that would burn. Four of the huge, grey canisters could be carried internally, leaving the wing pylons free for napalm or, most commonly, conventional iron bombs.

The M35 or M36 designation depended upon the number of sub-munitions inside, but the bomb casing itself remained the same size and looked identical. Essentially, the M35 was considered a 750-lb weapon and the M36 a 1000-lb weapon. The bomb's thin, four-finned shell was blasted open by a strip of Primacord that ran lengthwise between the two halves of the canister. Inside were as many as 152 long, thin bomblets, whose fins popped out as they were scattered into an area about the size of a football pitch. When the nose of the bomblet hit the ground, a fuse set off a white phosphorous charge that shot flaming napalm out the rear of the weapon over a circle about two metres in diameter. There were enough bomblets in each bomb so that they overlapped one another's fire, creating a 'lake' of incredibly hot flame that adhered to everything it touched and was virtually impossible to extinguish.

Retired Maj Gen Bill Maxson was a young major when he flew B-57s in Vietnam, and he recalled, 'The M35 and M36 munitions were left over from World War 2. We understood that they were developed to attack Japanese cities and start fires as an incendiary weapon. They were never used in this role, however, and they had remained stored on Guam since VJ Day. They were refurbished for the Vietnam War and, as far as I know during my own tour, we were the only outfit using them. They were very effective as an area weapon, spreading out among the trucks and setting them on fire. Indeed, this munition was what made the B-57 such a formidable "truck killer". It was not an exaggeration that on some of our very successful sorties, one of our Canberras would achieve results greater than an entire squadron of F-100 or F-4 fighter-bombers.'

According to Maxson, when the supply of bombs finally ran out overall accuracy in truck killing suffered. However, the M35/36s were still being used after the B-57Bs were gone and the B-57G had arrived in late 1969. It is likely that another large cache of these bombs was located in a USAF warehouse somewhere.

Besides bombs and the occasional load of rockets, the B-57s had their wing guns for strafing. As previously mentioned, the early machines off the production line mounted four 0.50-cal machine guns in each wing, while the later blocks carried two 20 mm cannon per wing. Each pilot had a preference for which type of guns he preferred to fight with, although the majority leaned toward the more versatile 20 mm weapons. The types of rounds they carried varied from plain 0.50-cal 'slugs' or 'ball' ammunition to combinations of armour-piercing incendiary (API) or high-explosive incendiary (HEI), the latter ones mostly available in 20 mm rounds.

The guns were optimised for strafing, being depressed by three

Armourers attach tail fuses to M35/36 incendiary cluster bomb units, universally known as 'funny bombs'. The bomb canisters split open after being dropped, spreading napalm and phosphorous bomblets over an area the size of a football pitch, with each bomblet shooting a jet of jellied flame out the rear as it struck the ground, causing fires that were virtually impossible to extinguish. The bombs, originally intended for use in the aborted invasion of the Japanese Home Islands, had been stored in a warehouse on Guam since the end of World War 2. The B-57 (and possibly the B-26 Invader) was the only aircraft to carry these bombs in the Vietnam War, where they were heavily used on trucks and troops on the Ho Chi Minh trail (*John DeCillo*)

degrees so that attack runs could be done in a shallower dive, giving more coverage of the target.

According to 8th BS pilot Capt Ed Rider, 'The 20 mm were all HEI and the 0.50-cals were all API. I think the tracers were loaded every tenth round. When I became weapons officer, I tried to get the 20 mm ammo changed to 50 percent HEI and 50 percent API because the HEI did not completely destroy trucks – it just blew the external sheet metal off. I have strafed a truck one day with 20 mm HEI and come back the next day and it was gone. If I strafed a truck with 0.50-cal API you could see it collapsing as the axles, motor and transmission were taken apart. I never did get any 20 mm API. HEI is great if you are shooting at aircraft made of thin aluminium and full of fuel'.

One negative point against the 20 mm cannons was that they had to be armed by groundcrew just before the aircraft positioned for take-off, or in the arming area. The 0.50-cal weapons could not only be charged from the cockpit, they could also be recharged by the pilot in flight in order to clear a jam – the 20 mm weapons could not. Jammed guns often meant going home with almost a full load of ammunition.

'The 0.50s could be armed in the air and that is why I always made sure that only 0.50 cal-equipped jets were used on alert', Rider explained. 'When we pulled alert at Phan Rang with the F-100s, and we were both scrambled at the same time, the B-57s would be at the end of the runway ready to take off before the Super Sabres got to the arming area to get their 20s armed.

'When we reached the jet we would climb up the ladder and reach in and turn on the battery, push both throttles to idle and hit both start switches. By the time we were strapped in we had enough power to pull out of the chocks. The napalm (safing) pins were pulled just before we left the chocks. Then the tower would give us a green light for take-off because the old tube ARC-27 UHF radio would not be warmed up by the time we reached the end of the runway, thus making it impossible to get communication from the tower except via coloured lights. We were usually airborne in under five minutes from the alert. We often reached the target, dropped our bombs and met the F-100s on the way home!'

BARREL ROLL AND STEEL TIGER

The Ho Chi Minh Trail, with its network of trunk routes, larger arteries and tiny trails branching off from Laos into South Vietnam, was virtually impossible to map accurately, especially since the routes changed constantly. And when main routes were cut by bombing, they were often repaired overnight by crews of peasants who were impressed at gunpoint into road gangs.

The 'Trail', as the whole network was called, was divided into tactical zones, with all of northern Laos coming under the codename *Barrel Roll*,

After assembly, the 'funny bombs' were loaded aboard the Martin bomb delivery system that was unique to American Canberras. As can clearly be seen here, the M35/36 bombs were attached directly to the rotary bomb door, which in this case is shown half-open. The door swung over 180 degrees, exposing the bombs to the slipstream. The system was designed for use both in level or dive-bombing attacks (*John DeCillo*)

while *Steel Tiger* covered the country's southern panhandle. Later, the *Steel Tiger* area was carved up into even more subdivisions near the Demilitarised Zone (DMZ), with these stretches being codenamed *Cricket* and *Tiger Hound*. They were created as the interdiction programme became larger and larger. However, in the early days, the Canberras were assigned to both *Barrel Roll* and *Steel Tiger* targets, and these formed the bulk of their assignments.

The first *Steel Tiger* mission – which officially did not exist as far as the press and public were concerned – was fragged (tasked) for the night of 3 April 1965, with two B-57s being aided by a *Blind Bat* C-130 'flare ship'. The targets were spotted by FACs from military and quasi-military, CIA-controlled units such as the Raven FACs, Air America or USAF FACs who, like the B-57s and the 'flare ships', were in the area clandestinely. The Canberra units would fly these missions for the next seven years, interrupted only during the few months after the last of the B-57Bs departed – finally forced out by combat losses that could no longer be replaced from the US – and the time the new B-57Gs were being brought up to combat readiness in late 1969.

On 7 April 1965 the 8th BS lost its first crew in *Barrel Roll* when Capt Wimberley Lewis and his navigator, Capt Arthur Dale Baker, flew into the ground after their aircraft (53-3880) failed to recover from a dive-bombing run on a target on Route 7. On this mission, four B-57s had been fragged for an interdiction mission on the Trail in Xieng Khouang province. Despite a five-day search, no sign of the two crewmen was found, although the New China News Agency reported the aircraft as shot down about three miles northeast of Khang Kay.

The squadrons flew missions for another five weeks without incident, but when it finally came, it would be utterly devastating, and there would be no enemy to blame other than the inherent danger of modern warfare.

NIGHT TACTICS

The Canberra squadrons, which were always meant to eventually serve in the role of night intruders, were not able to conduct night operations 'by the book' for the simple reason that the book had not yet been written. So they had to do it themselves, mostly by trial and error. That is a deadly way to learn in wartime. Crews did have the experiences of the B-26 to inspire them, as the Douglas 'twin' interdicted everything from trucks to trains during the Korean War, and prominent among these were the Invaders of the 13th BS. However, veterans of the conflict were scarce in-theatre by the time Vietnam came around. Also, the tactics employed by jets differed from those of propeller-driven aircraft.

Nevertheless, the 8th and 13th BSs began flying night missions over North Vietnam on 21 April 1965. Since the C-130 'flare ships' were not cleared for operations 'up North', the B-57s, operating in pairs, had to carry their own Mk 24 flares, along with six 500-lb bombs internally and eight Mighty Mouse rocket pods containing seven 2.75-in FFARs each. One pilot compared the efficacy of the latter's 1.5-lb warhead to 'throwing rocks' at the enemy. The flash given off by the rockets also played havoc with the crews' night vision.

On that first night, attacks were made against a railway bridge and a concrete road bridge near Vinh, on the coast of southern North Vietnam.

Crews encountered heavy flak around the targets, although they all returned safely to Da Nang for refuelling prior to flying back to Bien Hoa. According to Robert Mikesh, only six of these night missions over the North were flown over the next several weeks, and they did not become part of the squadrons' normal 'routine' until the move to Da Nang. Still, the sorties left a distinct impression on those who flew them, and it was here that the seeds of the DOOM Pussy legend were sown.

In theory, at least, crews were supposed to be thoroughly checked out in night operations before they were turned loose to head out on their own hunting trips. However, this checkout period, and the training that went with it, was often cut short due to a lack of qualified pilots and instructors. Crews were still getting to grips with the night mission when the squadrons moved to Da Nang in late June 1965.

Capt Robert 'Bat' Bateman was one such individual rushed through the night combat qualification 'syllabus' due to the lack of pilots and instructors;

'The 8th and 13th BSs alternated deployments from Clark to Da Nang every 60 days. When I began my first combat tour, the requirements for a crew to fly night interdiction missions were to have completed a night bombing checkout on a range in the Philippines, flown a minimum of 50 day-combat missions and undertaken three night bombing checkout sorties with an instructor pilot.

'However, the pace of night operations generated a need for far more missions to be flown than the squadrons had pilots to accomplish them. There was a job to be done. None of the new guys from Training Command had completed the night bombing on the Clark range. We each had about 25 missions. The solution was simple – waive the training mission at Clark and reduce the required day missions to 25. We still had to fly three night missions with an instructor though. This soon proved to be more difficult than anyone had imagined.

'The first problem was the weather (not an unusual situation). It was so bad that on my first two scheduled night missions all we could do was fly a "Sky Dump". This is a ground radar-controlled bomb run at over 20,000 ft – straight and level, and release when the controller says to. It is not exactly what the "top brass" had in mind when they decided that three night missions would be required before we were qualified to drop bombs in a 30- to 45-degree dive under flares.

'On my third night mission the weather cleared, the flares were dropped, a target was identified and I was able to unload a full load of 500-lb bombs on a major road trail. There were a few rounds of AAA fired at us as we pulled back into the darkness and went home to Da Nang. What a night. I was now

Piling on the Gs in a tight turn, this 13th BS B-57B enters the Bien Hoa traffic pattern upon returning from a combat mission. One difference between the Martin B-57B and the British Canberra was the fuselage-mounted 'speed board' type airbrakes, used in conjunction with the unique English Electric-designed 'finger' type airbrakes on either wing. American Canberras needed more drag-producing surfaces because the USAF utilised dive-bombing as its standard method of tactical delivery. Note the prodigious black residue left by gun gas during strafing runs on the wings of this 0.50-cal-armed aircraft (*Bob Galbreath*)

This could be the iconic photograph of the early days of US military involvement in Southeast Asia, with 8th BS B-57Bs parked wing-to-wing in the open, bombs scattered on the ground between them. The aircraft are not camouflaged, nor are there any protective revetments. In the background are VNAF A-1E Skyraiders and in the distance US Army UH-1 Huey helicopters depart Bien Hoa in close trail, heading for a landing zone somewhere out in the bush (*George Rose*)

fully qualified as a night pilot, having logged three night combat missions. On paper, I was ready to go. I flew five more night missions on that (60-day) deployment. When the squadron got back to Clark, they scheduled me for a training mission on the night bombing range!'

Ed Rider recalled that he actually enjoyed night combat missions;

'It really helped that I was very good at instrument flying, so night dive-bombing and strafing did not present any problem. We soon discovered that keeping track of the other aeroplane made formation night attacks impractical, so we were each assigned our own area and had it to ourselves. It was up to us to find our targets.

'I was assigned a good gung ho navigator in the form of Jim Coffey, who always carried an excellent pair of binoculars with him that he had bought in Japan. We had pretty good luck finding trucks running with battle lights, and after a few two-month tours I was quite proficient. In fact my nav and I racked up lots of truck kills. There was one method we used that I never shared with the other pilots. In fact, a lot of the tactics I used I did not share! The pilots who replaced the old pros were not as good, and I did not want to be responsible for getting them killed.

'Jim Coffey and I came up with a method to strafe trucks on the road if there was a half-moon or more. In the daytime I experimented to find out at what altitude and airspeed my guns would harmonise on one point. The guns were supposed to harmonise at 3200 ft. We found that 300 ft and 230 knots was the secret. A lot of the roads in Pac One near the coast were made of white sand. I would turn out all my cockpit lights and Jim would unplug all his except his altimeter. I would let down away from the roads and set my power for 230 knots and Jim would talk me down until I established myself at 300 ft. When I got comfortable there, he would turn out his altimeter light. The idiot would then unstrap and get out of his parachute and crawl up to get his head as close to mine so that he too could see out of the front windscreen!

'We would drive down the roads looking for dark places in the white sand. We often got shot at by flak guns off to the side of the road, but they were firing at sound. With the engines at such a low setting, they always fired above us. When I saw a dark spot, I waited until it was just short of where I knew my pipper would be and closed my eyes to avoid losing my night vision from the muzzle flash. Then I fired a three-second burst. I opened my eyes and made a hard break to the right because the guns would shoot at where they thought I would be. We sometimes shot at tree shadows, but were very often rewarded by seeing a truck go up in flames and then get multiple explosions. The best one was a fuel tanker that lit up the whole countryside.'

When the annual monsoon seasons rolled in, and cloud cover often obscured the targets, the B-57 crews (and the other tactical bomber units) were ordered to participate in a level bombing technique that used the MSQ-77 *Combat Sky Spot* system. The target would be located using several ground radar stations set up in South Vietnam and Laos, and the data would be processed by an EB-66 (or other aircraft) leading the formation. Upon the leader's signal, all the jets would drop their bombs at once. This method was disparagingly called 'Sky Dump' by the Canberra crews in reference to the fact that they were simply 'dumping' their bombs in the blind with little chance of hitting anything important.

'When the weather was too lousy to take off and find the targets, we were sometimes scheduled to join up with an EB-66 that had radar bombing capability', recalled Capt Bateman. 'A flight of four B-57s, two on each wing, would accompany the EB-66 on a bomb run from high altitude – 20,000 ft or above. The EB-66 radar-navigator would conduct a bombing run on a target such as a ferry point or storage area, and call out when to release our bombs. For some reason the EB-66 loaded with electronic gear did not carry its own bombs.

'On one of these missions, the EB-66 crew made a mistake and began leading the flight out over a SAM-infested area without finding the target. There was a break in the clouds, and the EB-66 pilot saw the coast and the SAM area just ahead. Somewhat concerned, he began an immediate left turn, banking to about 60 degrees. Now, he had two aircraft on each wing, and this sudden turn caused the two aircraft on the

A pair of 8th BS B-57Bs unload a mixture of 750- and 500-lb bombs after receiving the signal to drop from an escorting EB-66 during a *Combat Sky Spot* mission. When targets were obscured by low cloud, rain or fog, the radar-directed *Sky Spot* missions were often ordered, and these were carried out at altitudes in excess of 20,000 ft while flying straight and level. Although Australian Canberra B 20 crews achieved good results with *Combat Sky Spot*, their USAF counterparts did not, and they disparagingly referred to it as 'Sky Dump' because they felt they were randomly dumping their bombs far from their target (*Vern Wittkopp*)

A crewman heads for his aircraft at the start of yet another mission from Bien Hoa in the spring of 1965. B-57B 53-3904 is loaded with 750-lb napalm canisters under the wings and 500-lb general purpose bombs in the bay. This jet, along with nine more Canberras and other aircraft, would be destroyed in the Bien Hoa ramp explosion a few weeks after this photograph was taken. During this time missions were being flown at such a frenetic pace that bombs were commonly brought from the dump and left between aircraft so they could be turned around quickly for the next mission

inside of the turn to have to pull throttles to idle, duck down under the EB-66 and slide to the outside of the turn (usually while uttering mild oaths). At the same time, the two on the outside of the turn had to add full power and ride high to avoid the unexpected arrival of the inside team. Ever concerned with safety, the affected crews diverted their attention away from keeping a tight formation and became more focused on avoiding the multiple opportunities for collisions that were sure to arise.

'In this case the result was five aircraft scattered to the four winds, all heading away from the target area at high power settings. It took half-an-hour for everyone to find the EB-66 leader and line up for another bomb run. Yes, we lined up and did it all again until being given the signal for "Bombs away!". We then headed for home, all breathing a little easier.

'Anyway, that's why we called it "Sky Dump", because we released all of our ordnance at one time and had no idea where it would go.'

HOLOCAUST AT BIEN HOA

By the late spring of 1965, the two squadrons had fallen into the daily grind of flying combat missions, tropical weather allowing. Despite its use as a night intruder, the B-57 was by no means an all-weather bomber. Nevertheless, day in and day out the Canberra ramp was an anthill of activity, with vehicles coming and going and all manner of bombs and rockets being moved from here to there before being uploaded, along with belt after belt of 20 mm and 0.50-cal ammunition.

In any air combat situation, the opportunities for disaster lurk in every action taken by those who work on the ramp or fly the aeroplanes.

16 May 1965 would go down as the blackest day in the history of both Canberra squadrons. During this time the B-57s were still regularly flying in flights of four, eight and occasionally even 16 aircraft. On this day, the morning flights were already departing for their targets, with 'Paget' Flight having begun taxiing out at 0800 hrs. The three remaining aircraft from 'Jade' Flight, led by Capt Charlie Fox and his navigator, Capt Vern Haynes, were just starting engines at 0815 hrs prior to flying a 'secret war' mission to Laos – such flights were identified by gemstone call-signs.

With no warning whatsoever, 'Jade' Flight lead exploded with a horrendous concussion, sending debris over the ramp and setting off an almost simultaneous chain reaction that sent a fiery, boiling mushroom cloud high into the air. The dead, dying and wounded lay sprawled for acres around. Each of the 'Jade' Flight aircraft, along with others on the ramp, was loaded with four 750-lb bombs under the wings and nine old World War 2-vintage 500-lb bombs in the bays, and all but one had gone up. Other bombs stacked on the runway also cooked off, as did belts of ammunition, both 0.50-cal and 20 mm HEI rounds. A complete Wright

Although of poor quality, this is the only known photograph of the moment the flightline at Bien Hoa exploded in a hellish mixture of bombs, 20 mm ammunition, fuel bladders and aircraft. Ten B-57s and 11 VNAF A-1H Skyraiders were destroyed, along with a transient US Navy F-8E Crusader whose USAF exchange pilot was killed in the blast, and a lone USAF HH-43 Huskie helicopter. An additional 26 USAF personnel were also killed, many instantly, and 105 more people were injured. The VNAF also suffered a significant number of casualties. The cause of the blast was believed to be a damaged time-delay fuse fitted to a 500-lb GP bomb loaded onto one of a flight of three aircraft that was preparing to start engines for a mission. The photograph was shot with a small 16 mm camera by navigator Capt Dick Fontaine, who was sitting in the back seat of a Canberra at the end of the active runway just getting ready to roll (*Richard Fontaine*)

Armourers finish attaching a quartet of 750-lb M117s to the underwing pylons of B-57B 52-1530. A further nine 500-lb GP bombs have already been uploaded into the jet's bomb-bay. This jet was taken from a Kentucky ANG unit after the attack on the base at Bien Hoa, and the tail still shows where the ANG insignia was hastily removed. 52-1530 was lost with both crewmen during a daylight mission over Laos on 7 April 1966 (*via John DeCillo*)

J65 turbojet engine from one of the aircraft was found half-a-mile away and large chunks of metal were hurled almost a mile into the base housing area.

Capt Art Jepson and his navigator, 1Lt Lee Wagner, also from 'Jade' Flight, were strapped into their aircraft parked next to Fox and Haynes. Both Jepson and Wagner died instantly, as did the lead crew. Capt Howard Greene in 'Jade' Flight's No 4 jet, along with his navigator, Lt John Burbank, were at the far eastern end of the ramp awaiting start-up when the explosion went off. After ducking debris, the men jumped from their aircraft and survived the holocaust. Meanwhile, USAF jet fuel, known as JP-4, stored in 50,000-gallon rubber bladders above ground, ruptured and sent a deluge of burning kerosene washing over the already hellish scene.

USAF Maj R G Bell, who was an exchange pilot with US Navy fighter squadron VF-162 embarked in the USS *Oriskany* (CVA-34), had diverted his malfunctioning F-8E Crusader to Bien Hoa mid-mission, and he had landed just moments before the explosion. Bell was killed as he walked near his jet. It has been said that the appearance of the F-8 – not a common sight at the base – had saved some lives because it had attracted groundcrew away from the main flightline out of curiosity.

Navigator Lt Barry Knowles and his pilot Capt Andrew M Kea, who had ground aborted while starting up as part of 'Paget' Flight, were walking away from their jet when the explosion occurred. Kea was killed instantly by flying shrapnel, but Knowles was knocked to the ground, having suffered severe cuts to his face, temporarily blinding him. He was picked up and driven to safety by Snr MSgt Leon Adamson, who had himself suffered serious burns and numerous wounds from debris and shrapnel. It was only one of many heroic acts that occurred that morning.

'Paget' Flight, which was still departing when the explosion happened, pressed on and completed its mission, after which it was diverted to Tan Son Nhut. Debris covered the entire base, including the runway.

In the end, 27 USAF men were killed in the disaster. No fewer than ten B-57s had been destroyed, along with a USAF A-1E and a Kaman HH-43 Huskie rescue helicopter, a US Navy F-8E and 11 VNAF Skyraiders. A further 20 VNAF A-1s were damaged to some degree. It would remain as the worst disaster of the war for the USAF.

An extensive investigation followed, even as the squadrons began recuperating and returning to limited operations from Tan Son Nhut.

1Lt Fleming Hobbs suspected that a faulty delayed-action fuse had caused the accident;

'These particular fuses were only available for the 500-lb box fin bombs. Modern fuses become active so many seconds (which is settable) after release through a propeller that spins down in the airstream. At that time a "mask" moves away from the firing pin. Prior to that, if two bombs collide or hit anything, the pin hits the "mask" and no detonation.

'The delayed fuses were only in the tail of the 500-lb bombs. On those, the impact broke a glass vial of acetone that started to eat away on a washer that held back a firing pin. Depending upon the temperature, six, 12, or 24 hours later the bomb went off. In order to make sure that the chemical vial was not broken before you inserted the fuse into the bomb, you did a "sniff test" to tell if the fuse was "ticking". In my opinion that was the source of the ground accident at Bien Hoa.

'Bombs were fused on the flightline. It is likely that a six-hour bomb in the heat blew at about four hours when all the aircraft were parked together. It could just as easily have gone off in the air 30 minutes later. As I recall, that was a 16-aircraft mission. Four had taken off, four were at the end of the runway, four crews were sitting in their aircraft waiting for a start and four crews were walking to their aircraft. There were no revetments, so everything went up.

'To make matters worse, we used so many bombs that they couldn't get enough of them (from the bomb dump) during the day to load up jets for afternoon missions after the morning missions had come back.

This diagram of the ramp at Bien Hoa was produced by the USAF Accident Review Board. It shows where all the aircraft were, their flight number and their weapons load when the base was devastated by exploding ordnance on the morning of 16 May 1965. The red circles show where the bodies of those killed were found (*USAF*)

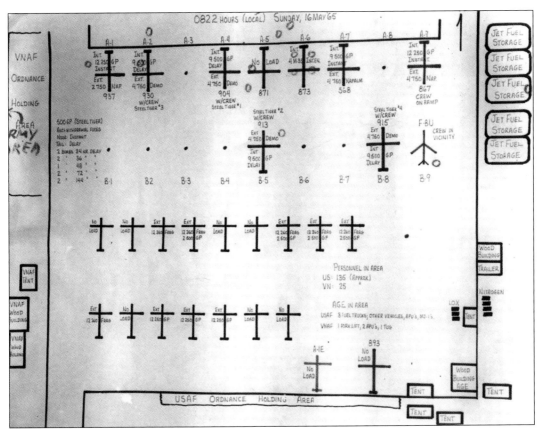

So armourers stacked 500 "pounders" in between the aircraft on the ramp. Now these things were perfectly safe. Indeed, you could drop a Composition B-loaded 500 "pounder" on concrete and it wouldn't go off. And the Tritinol used in the more modern 750 "pounders" was even safer. But let an explosion occur, and throw hot fragments into a 500 "pounder", and it would go off.'

Maj Pete Hall witnessed the explosion;

'Well, the way the older fuses were made, if you dropped them on the ground they were dangerous. And that day while we prepared for a mission, a bomb went off spontaneously and aircraft were going off one after the other down the flightline. Somebody had dropped one of those fuses (breaking the vial of solvent), then put it in a bomb, which went off by itself after that. It turned out to be a case of inadequate training. These kids had never loaded anything other than "nukes", so they couldn't handle conventional ordnance during this early time in the war quite as efficiently.'

An extensive investigation was launched, and as Hobbs, Hall and many others among the air- and groundcrews had suspected, it came to the conclusion that somehow a 'ticking' time-delay fuse had been put into a bomb that was loaded aboard an aircraft scheduled for the afternoon mission. It was even suspected that the fuse had been taken from a classroom, where it was a teaching aid, and used in a bomb scheduled to be dropped by 'Jade' Flight, although this was doubted by many of the armourers. In fairness, these armourers strongly objected to suggestions that they would be so inattentive as to load a damaged fuse.

Pilot Don Nation was a member of the accident board that investigated the disaster;

'All of the B-57s had full fuel and ordnance loads of various denominations, and so there were a number of sympathetic explosions. We failed to reach an agreement on what the hell made the first one blow up. There *was* one thing I learned for certain. The worst witnesses are the "eye" ones. There was one crew chief who was standing facing his aircraft when the aeroplane directly behind him exploded and sent him flying forward. He ended up underneath his jet. His injuries were quite serious, but were all to his backside, not frontal injuries other than some scrapes and bruises from rolling across the concrete. Yet when I talked to him a few years later he still swore up and down that it was his aeroplane that exploded, and not the one directly behind him!'

For some reason, the 'brass' failed to embrace the accident board's recommendation that aircraft should not be parked in the open, wing to wing, as they had been through two disasters now. It was never explained why the PACAF did not address the very conspicuous fact that after the mortar attack on 1 November 1964 no revetments had been built to keep the aircraft separate from one another, and in fact little or nothing had been done to make the ramp a safer place for men and materiel.

The two squadrons were immediately moved to temporary, primitive quarters at busy Tan Son Nhut airport on the outskirts of Saigon. Meanwhile, yet more aircraft were immediately requisitioned from stateside ANG units to replace those lost in the Bien Hoa disaster. These older aircraft joined the other early B-57Bs that had been brought over after the mortar attack six-and-a-half months earlier.

DA NANG

By the early summer of 1965 Tan Son Nhut airport was bursting at the seams. The vast complex of runways, hangars, shops, barracks and administrative buildings were home to everything from commercial airline flights to USAF F-102 Delta Dagger interceptors sitting in their alert barns. There was also a CIA U-2 compound on the airfield, and pretty well everything else besides. And that did not include the VNAF facilities which took up much of the field, located just outside of Saigon.

So when the 8th and 13th BSs were moved there after the 15 May tragedy, they were accommodated at the edge of the airport in a patch of mud and grass festooned with hastily thrown-up facilities. Some crews were even billeted with a neighbouring US Army helicopter unit. Aircraft were parked on pierced steel planking hardstands and maintenance took place either in the open air or, in some cases, on the grass. Such was the weather that the skin on the aircraft often became too hot to touch before midday. Yet round-the-clock B-57 strike operations were expected to take place at their usual frenetic pace without interruption.

The two squadrons had been at Tan Son Nhut for less than two weeks when they lost their first aeroplane to enemy fire. On 8 June 1965 four Canberras were on a CAS mission in the Mekong Delta, just west of Can Tho, when the No 4 aircraft in the flight, B-57B 53-3882 of the 13th BS, was hit by ground fire as it pulled off its third bombing pass. After the left wing caught fire, pilot Capt Gordon F Nelson activated the engine fire extinguisher, which failed to douse the flames. Suspecting the fire was in the wing fuel tank, and therefore might well burn through the wing, Nelson and his navigator, Capt James R Carnes, ejected. Before their feet touched the ground US Army UH-1 Huey helicopter gunships were on the scene providing covering fire to protect the crewmen, while their three remaining flight mates circled overhead. One of the Hueys picked up both men less than five minutes after they had landed. Meanwhile, the three B-57s destroyed the 0.50-cal machine gun position that was suspected of downing Nelson and Carnes, who were unhurt.

Eleven days later a second Canberra was lost, and the crew was not so fortunate this time. On 19 June Capt Charles Kennedy Lovelace and his backseater, Capt William Edward Cordero, of the 8th BS were flying 53-3910 as a pathfinder fighter-bomber – a mission the B-57s performed occasionally because they had the navigational advantage of a two-man crew. While leading the jets over the southernmost province of North Vietnam, Lovelace and Cordero crashed and were killed. It was never determined whether they were lost to AAA, equipment failure or other reasons. Their bodies were not recovered until after the war.

One thing that made the arrangement at Tan Son Nhut only slightly more bearable was the B-57 itself. The aircraft, thanks to its simplicity, was not as maintenance-intensive as the F-4 Phantom II or the F-105 Thunderchief. In fact, the B-57 did not even require the large and unwieldy yellow starter carts that were ubiquitous on USAF airfields everywhere. The Canberra's two J65 engines were started using black-powder cartridges that were clipped in place inside the bullet fairing in the middle of the intakes. These cartridges emitted so much black smoke that the uninitiated thought the aircraft was on fire. When an entire flight was starting engines, it became so smoky on the ramp that it was difficult to see. The smoke belched from an exhaust hole on the side of the engine nacelle.

Each jet carried four spare starter cartridges in a bay for that purpose in the rear of the aircraft. Sometimes, when hit by AAA, the cartridges would ignite, and this led to an order banning their carriage in combat.

Very soon it was clear that the two squadrons' situation at Tan Son Nhut was untenable (and for the crews billeted there, unbearable). Operations could simply not be sustained under the primitive conditions forced upon the units, where the slapdash setup was particularly hard on both the maintenance personnel and armourers. Any notion of the two squadrons returning to Bien Hoa was out of the question, so a new base was soon settled upon by the command. After a number of delays, from 18 June through to early July the two units moved to the expanding US Marine Corps base at Da Nang, located in I Corps in northern South Vietnam. This move also meant that the B-57s were now closer to the targets in North Vietnam that the 8th BS was hitting at night.

The command structure over the two squadrons throughout the war was a confusing thing that was prone to change. At Clark, the 8th and 13th BSs came under the control of the 405th TFW, while at Da Nang they were assigned to the 6252nd TFW (the latter would become the 35th TFW on 8 April 1966). The latter was a composite outfit that also had two F-100 squadrons under its command. The wing at Clark had a detachment of F-102s, F-100s and half a squadron of T-33 jet trainers for staff officer proficiency flying and instrument currency. There were also various hacks and other assorted types under its responsibility.

Now, following this base move, orders were changed so that each of the two B-57 squadrons was rotated from Clark AFB to Da Nang and

A pair of 13th BS B-57Bs return to Da Nang after a strike mission in the Mekong Delta region of South Vietnam. This area was long a VC stronghold, and as more and more B-57 missions were flown at night over the Ho Chi Minh Trail and North Vietnam, the Royal Australian Air Force took over much of the fight over the Delta when No 2 Sqn arrived in 1967 with its Canberra B 20s

Any time a B-57 was started, it was a smoky, sooty affair. Here, the alert jet is starting both engines simultaneously using black-powder cartridges to 'spin the engines up' to starting RPM. The cartridges were used to start the B-57s virtually every time, and spares were initially carried in a special bay in the fuselage, which created quite a fire hazard in combat. This aircraft is armed with four finned napalm bombs on the pylons and 500-lb general purpose weapons in the bomb-bay. The jet's camouflage is interesting because of how high up the fuselage the underside light grey has been painted (*John DeCillo*)

A 13th BS B-57B undergoes routine maintenance between sorties in its revetment at Da Nang. Jets were often swapped from one squadron to the next, and the faded red paint on this one shows that it is a former 8th BS aircraft. The B-57B series was without question a simple, tough, no-frills aircraft, and maintenance complaints were few compared to jets like the complicated F-4 Phantom II (*via John DeCillo*)

This newly camouflaged B-57B, carrying a full load of eight 750-lb M117 general purpose bombs, has its bomb-bay open and is preparing to roll in on its target. At this time, the B-57 flightlines at Da Nang and Clark AFB were a hodgepodge of natural metal and camouflaged machines, some with light grey undersides and others painted black like this jet for better cover during the increasingly frequent DOOM Pussy night missions into North Vietnam and along the Ho Chi Minh Trail in Laos (*Bob Galbreath*)

back every 60 days. They would remain in the Philippines for 30 or 60 days. For every day pilots and navigators spent in the combat zone, 1.5 days were deducted from their tours. Most aircrew flew at least 45 missions per rotation.

Most USAF personnel in-theatre were sent for one-year tours, after which they were rotated to another post, unless they applied for, and were granted, an extension of their tour. Many did, for second, third and even fourth tours. But the one-year tour was mandatory, as it was with most aircrew serving in Southeast Asia. However, the 60-day temporary duty (TDY) arrangement observed by the B-57 squadrons was rare, if not unique, among USAF units in Southeast Asia. Most units that operated under TDY orders were "spook" outfits, usually detachments (DETs) with special, usually secret, missions. These included U-2 operations, US Navy and USAF sensor seeding units that flew along the Ho Chi Minh Trail and even stranger, sometimes experimental, squadrons like the US Navy's OP-2E Neptune sensor seeding/attack outfit VO-67, which suffered three combat losses in January-February 1968 and was withdrawn four months later.

When the 13th BS was at Da Nang, the 8th would fly training missions in the Philippines at the Crow Valley gunnery and bombing range right near the base, honing their skills, trying out new tactics and occasionally new weapons (although the same weapons were used pretty much from beginning to end). Then, upon rotation, the 13th would do the same while the 8th returned to combat at Da Nang.

The Crow Valley range was enormous, and crews had plenty of room to manoeuvre. They also used a nearby rocky outcrop in the sea as a bombing target. It was at Crow Valley that new crews were broken in prior to being sent into combat. Many of these 'FNGs' had been flying other types such as the B-47, the last of which were being phased out of the inventory, or B-57Es in the target tug or ECM training roles. These individuals had to be taught how to fight an air war, and the pilots in particular had to become familiar with the fine art of dive-bombing, which made up – by some pilots' estimates – as much as 95 percent of the B-57's workload in Vietnam.

Following the move to Da Nang, it was not long before the 8th BS was back to business as usual – an endless cycle of mostly night interdiction missions along the trail, mixed with armed reconnaissance missions over South Vietnam and CAS for troops in the field. And then there were the dreaded night sorties into North Vietnam, the DOOM Pussy missions.

8th BS CO Lt Col 'Red' Dan Farr, left, is seen here with his navigator, Capt William 'Pappy' Boyington, at Tan Son Nhut shortly after Farr took command of the squadron in the chaos following the 16 May 1965 holocaust at Bien Hoa. Of note here is Boyington's mostly cobbled-together survival kit, which dangles down to his knees. At this early stage of the war the USAF had not yet come up with a good survival kit appropriate for the jungle and mountain environment in which most crewmen found themselves upon ejecting. Note the No 2 Sqn RAAF kangaroo 'zap' stencilled onto the jet to the right of Lt Col Farr's left hand (*via William Boyington*)

Captured NVA and VC prisoners had an especial hatred for the Canberras, which was expressed when the prisoners were shown silhouettes of various American aircraft. The B-57 engine had a whine unlike any other aircraft, and the VC insurgents and NVA regulars learned when they heard that sound that trouble was coming. They despised the Canberras for the same reason they dreaded the old and slow A-1 Skyraiders – both aircraft could operate over an area for hours, and could carry a huge load of ordnance compared to other fighter-bombers. Also, their slower speed and steadiness in the air made them deadly accurate in both bombing and strafing.

Around this time the B-57s, which had been operating in the same natural metal finish they had worn in Korea, with a red or yellow nose cap and diagonal band just behind the fuselage to identify the squadron, got a coat of war paint. At first, the jets were painted in the standard Southeast Asia camouflage, which consisted of two shades of green and one of tan on the uppersurfaces and pale grey undersides. However, because more and more of their missions were being flown at night, the undersides were eventually painted a matt to semi-gloss black.

Coinciding with the adoption of camouflage was the arrival of new 8th BS CO, Lt Col Dan Farr, who had flown P-47 Thunderbolts in World War 2 and F-51 Mustangs during the Korean War. A highly competent aviator, he could make a B-57 'stand on its hind legs and bark' according to one of his pilots. Farr's crews, from young enlisted men to veteran combat pilots, looked upon him with a respect that bordered on veneration. One B-57 'driver' referred to the ginger-haired Farr (also known as 'Red Dan') as 'the pilot's pilot'. He was almost as a big a legend in the B-57 community as the DOOM Pussy itself. Farr could be distinguished in the air by his personal Canberra, which was waxed to a mirror-finish and bore no squadron markings or colours other than a green shamrock and the legend *Liz + 3*, referring to his wife and children. The same art had appeared on Farr's Mustang in Korea. He even inspired one of his young pilots, Capt Robert 'Bat' Bateman, to write the following poem in his honour;

The Commander
He was tall and he was tough, and we all knew well enough he'd a heart as big as all the sky he flew in.
Though his grin was big and wide, he was tough as nails inside, and was always in the lead when trouble's brewin'.
In the briefing room one day, he stood up to have his say. By the time he'd done, the room was mighty quiet. 'We have just two jobs to do before

this fight is through, and they both need your good plane and you to fly it.'

'Now your first job is to kill, 'til the VC get their fill. If you cannot first do this, don't mind the other. For the second is "Come back". Damn the MiGs and Damn the flak. Let's have every last man Jack come back to Mother.'

'At the root of every war are some things worth fighting for. There are some things that we say are worth the trying. But if someone has to die, let's make it the other guy, for a victory here is more than worth the trying.'

Farr's backseater, Capt William 'Pappy' Boyington, was himself a larger-than-life character and was as two-fisted, tough and beloved among the B-57 community as Farr himself.

Farr and Boyington showed some of that willingness to do things above and beyond the call of duty on 27 July 1965 – a bad day for the USAF, which lost six F-105s over North Vietnam in quick succession. When reports reached Da Nang that 'Thud' pilot Capt Frank J Tullo of the 12th TFS/18th TFW had safely ejected from his F-105D (62-4407) only 27 miles west of Hanoi, Farr and Boyington took off, with Lt Col Bob 'Whale' Smith and his navigator, Capt John Hughes, on their wing. It was just before 1700 hrs, and the two aircraft flew the length of North Vietnam to provide RESCAP (Rescue Combat Air Patrol) for the pilot.

As it happened, Tullo had floated down in an area thick with SAM and AAA sites, and this was the first time the B-57 was used in the rescue role – a task normally performed gallantly by the A-1 'Sandy' Skyraiders of the Air Commando units. The B-57s were vectored to the downed pilot's location by 'Panama', the ground radar station that covered the area, and they arrived overhead just 68 minutes after taking off. There, they orbited while awaiting the HH-3 Jolly Green Giant rescue helicopter, which had to refuel at *Lima* Site 36 in Laos before proceeding into North Vietnam. So far was this penetration – the farthest into North Vietnam to date for a rescue attempt – that the Jolly Green Giant crew, led by Capt George Martin, had no maps of the area. By now, two US Navy A-1 Skyraiders had also arrived on the scene.

Finally, with fuel running low, Farr reluctantly had to leave the scene and fly to Udorn Royal Thai Air Base (RTAB) to refuel. Another pair of B-57s had taken off 20 minutes after Farr, this flight being led by Maj Gail Manning with navigator Capt Phil Mason, while Capt Ken Blackwell and his backseater, Capt John Kendrick, flew on their wing. They were vectored to pick up the helicopter as it crossed into North Vietnam and provide escort to the downed pilot's location. Darkness was beginning to fall by now, and every minute Tullo

A groundcrewman prepares to refill the right wing tank of a B-57B at Da Nang. One of the biggest enemies of the groundcrews was the unrelenting weather – in this case, scorching heat. Often, the skin of the aircraft became too hot to touch with bare hands by midday

This aircraft, B-57E 55-4269, was a rare beast. Due to the dreadful Canberra attrition rate in Vietnam, in late 1965 the USAF directed Martin to convert early B-57Bs and a dozen newer B-57E target tugs to combat configuration. This is one of the latter, which was lost to a non-combat crash on 10 October 1971. The pilot, Capt Bob Butterfield, left, is shown with his navigator, Capt Roger Bauman, following a daylight mission. Both are wearing 13th BS 50-mission caps (*Bob Butterfield*)

remained on the ground the worse his chances of being successfully rescued became.

With the pilot located, the Jolly Green Giant crew attempted to hoist him aboard. It was at this critical moment that the B-57s began taking fire from nearby AAA locations. The hoist on the HH-3 jammed, leaving poor Tullo dangling by the cable, so during the egress the helicopter had to land in a clearing in order to get him safely inside. Mason and Blackwell, now in damaged aircraft that were flying literally on fumes, raced to Udorn and landed without a minute to spare.

Of the six F-105 pilots downed that day, Tullo was the only one who was not either killed or taken prisoner. The rescue was nothing short of amazing, and very few airmen shot down so close to Hanoi would ever make it out of North Vietnam.

THE RUNAWAY CANBERRA

On 6 August, just ten days after Capt Tullo's rescue, a bizarre and tragic episode occurred in the B-57 squadrons' own backyard. Capt Larry J Horacek and his navigator, 1Lt F William Johnson, were engaged in a daylight strike near the town of Nha Trang, on the central coast of South Vietnam. After taking heavy fire from the ground, Horacek found his aircraft (53-3919) virtually impossible to control. He had lost most or all electrical power and was unable to jettison his bombs.

Nevertheless, Horacek was able to wrestle the aircraft away from the town and onto a course out to sea before both men safely ejected just offshore. To the horror of his wingman, the stricken '919 began a gentle turn to the left and headed back toward Nha Trang (investigators later surmised that the turn was caused by the left engine flaming out from flak damage). The wingman got on the bomber's 'six-o'clock' position and attempted to shoot it down with his four 20 mm cannon while it was still over the ocean. However, the B-57's guns and sight were optimised for strafing, not air-to-air combat, and the guns themselves were depressed three degrees for this reason. The attempt was stopped when there was concern that the 20 mm rounds would hit the town.

In the event, it was the bomb-laden Canberra that hit the heart of Nha Trang instead, destroying dozens of shops as well as civilian homes. There were 14 civilians killed and 75 injured. If anything good could be said to have happened during this tragic incident, it is that only four of the 16 bombs aboard exploded in the crash, doubtless keeping the casualty count considerably less than it might have been. The crash strained relations between the local population and the US military, although the USAF did make restitution to those who lost property or loved ones in the accident.

Horacek would be shot down once more on 17 April 1966, and again he would 'turn to the silk' and be rescued uninjured.

Exactly one month after the Nha Trang disaster another B-57 was lost, but the outcome was much better this time. On 6 September 1965, the crew of 52-1544 suffered an engine failure during a CAS mission over South Vietnam and both men ejected. Capt W C Hamann and his back-seater, Capt R J Lane, were rescued without incident. Their aircraft was one of the nine early-production B-57Bs requisitioned from the Nevada ANG to replace those lost in the Bien Hoa disasters.

The next loss occurred on 20 October during the siege of the Plei Mei Special Forces Camp, which straddled the Laotian-South Vietnamese border about 80 miles west of Qui Nhon. These camps frequently came under attack due to their isolation from outside help, and because they caused so much trouble for the enemy. This was the most intense attack made against the camp so far in the war, with both NVA regulars and VC fighters being committed.

During the early hours of the 20th, two B-57s from the 'Yellowbirds' were scrambled from Da Nang to provide CAS to the beleaguered camp. Due to low cloud cover in the area, the B-57s bombed straight and level from altitudes that left them in danger of being downed by their own ordnance. The two-ship flight dumped 42 260-lb 'frags' and eight 500-lb GP bombs on the attackers, after which a number of strafing passes were made. It was a close-run thing since the bombers had to avoid friendlies, as well as being careful not to damage the base's airstrip – the lifeline of any Army Special Forces outpost.

These strikes held the attackers at bay long enough for the defenders to catch their breath, but by dawn the offensive was renewed. Two more Canberras were diverted from a strike mission north of Da Nang, and when they arrived at the camp a US Army UH-1 Huey helicopter and U-6 Beaver liaison and re-supply aircraft had been shot down.

The FAC working the area from his O-1 Bird Dog began spotting targets for the new flight of B-57s. The area surrounding Plei Mei Special Forces Camp was still blanketed in cloud, forcing crews to bomb from level flight at a slow airspeed. On his seventh strafing pass, having expended all his bombs, Maj Gerald T Hamilton, flying B-57B 53-3920, took fire from a 12.7 mm machine gun that ignited fuel in the starboard wingtip tank, blowing away a large section of wing. The other Canberra attacked the machine gun position and was itself hit and damaged.

Hamilton and his navigator, Maj Harold E Holzapple, turned toward Pleiku, although it quickly became apparent that the aircraft was no longer flyable. The pair ejected just before the aircraft crashed into the jungle. Landing safely, they were picked up by a helicopter that had been alerted as soon as the jet had departed the combat area. During the whole ordeal, the remaining damaged B-57 continued to orbit over the two men until they were aboard the rescue helicopter.

RANCH HAND

Among the many tasks given to the B-57s was the escorting of C-123s that were spraying defoliants over South Vietnam, including Agent Orange which would become such a 'hot-button' issue in the decades following the war. The defoliants were sprayed over areas where the VC were thought to be at their strongest, yet were proving hard to get at by conventional means.

As Robert Mikesh wrote, 'Americans, by nature, are not jungle fighters. To enhance our advantage to fight the war on our terms, the jungle growth along the enemy's supply routes was sprayed with defoliant, thus depriving him of this protective visual cover. These defoliation sorties were flown low and slow over some of the roughest terrain in the world for this type of flying. Hits from the ground were the rule rather than the exception'.

Whenever one of the C-123s began taking fire, it would toss out a smoke grenade marking the source of the shooting. The B-57s would then roll in on the flak site or machine gun, strafing and dropping 260-lb anti-personnel fragmentation bombs, of which each aeroplane could carry 21. It was quite common for the Canberras to return from these missions full of holes from small arms fire.

While performing *Ranch Hand* escorts B-57 crews inhaled a significant amount of the defoliant through their on-board environmental control systems. Several Canberra crewmen have died of leukaemia and lymphomas since the war, although the US government has refused to make a connection between these deaths and the *Ranch Hand* flights.

It was at around this time that both the 'Yellowbirds' and 'Redbirds' began flying the bulk of their missions at night from Da Nang following the development of tactics for bombing under flare light. Early on it was established that the B-57 was best utilised in night operations which, after all, was the original mission for which the American version of the Canberra was acquired. Unfortunately, no one thought to equip the aeroplane with the fundamental tools required for bombing at night, such as radar and advanced navigation systems.

In these early days, the trend was set with the B-57s usually flying singly or in pairs, although larger formations were not unheard of. After take-off, the Canberra crews would locate and join up with a C-130 'flare ship' using the call sign 'Blind Bat'. In the early days, this formation was made even more unusual through the addition of a US Marine Corps EF-10B Skyknight to provide ECM cover against radar-directed guns.

The first of thousands of *Steel Tiger* sorties over the Ho Chi Minh Trail in the panhandle of southern Laos was flown on the night of 3 April 1965 by two B-57s and a 'Blind Bat' C-130. At the time, these sorties were top secret, and mission details were not fully declassified until 1985. Most crew members and historians believe that more of the B-57's mission were classified as secret than were not due to the great number of sorties flown over Laos and, later, Cambodia.

It was at night that the trail came alive. The truck, foot and bicycle traffic slowed to a trickle during the day, but at night, under the cover of darkness and the thick jungle canopy, everything began to move. When the local FAC found a suspected target – this could be a convoy, a truck park, a supply dump or a simple enemy bivouac – the crew of the 'Blind Bat' C-130 would begin throwing out parachute flares, which illuminated the ground like daylight within the circle of their glow. The B-57 crew would note the location of the target and set up for a bombing or strafing run on it.

Bombing by flare light was a speciality all of its own, being as much art and instinct as science. Quite often the night itself became treacherous. Dr Robert 'Bat' Bateman, then a young captain, described one such mission;

Armourer John DeCillo is seen at Da Nang behind the wheel of an MJ-1 self-propelled bomb lift. These ubiquitous vehicles were found on virtually every air base in South Vietnam (*John DeCillo*)

This 8th BS B-57B is interesting for two reasons. Firstly, the worn yellow paint shows that in addition to the usual nose cap and intake bullets, the front of the wing tanks and the entire bomb pylons have been painted in the yellow squadron colour. Normally, when the B-57Bs wore natural metal finish, the tip tanks and underwing pylons were always painted matt black. Also, the jet is carrying non-finned 750-lb napalm bombs, which tumbled better than the finned bombs – tumbling was a desired characteristic as it spread the fiery jelly over a larger area (*Paul Searls*)

Above and Below
8th BS's 53-3908 was one of the rare natural metal finish aircraft with personal nose art. Christened *Miss MiNuki*, the jet had previously spent a relatively quiet life sitting alert with a nuclear warhead at Kunsan AB, in South Korea, prior to being sent to South Vietnam. 53-3908's nickname could, therefore, be taken two ways! Shown here in a revetment at Da Nang in January 1966, the aircraft was brought down by small arms fire just ten miles from its new base at Phan Rang, with the loss of both pilot Capt Elwin H Busch and his navigator, 1Lt Peter Whitcomb Morrison, on 8 June 1967 (*Robert Zelski*)

'It was a night interdiction mission over the trail from North Vietnam toward the south. We were looking for truck convoys carrying ammunition to the VC. The "Blind Bat" C-130 "flare ship" had located a group of trucks that had paused in a horseshoe bend in a river. There were a few clouds around, but the weather was basically VFR. They dropped a flare so that we would be able to see the river in its reflection.

'Doug (my navigator) and I rolled in to deliver, but the flare went out before we could get a fix on the trucks. We went back up to our "perch" and "Blind Bat" dropped another flare. Again we rolled in, but just as the target was coming within range a cloud came between us and the horseshoe bend. I rolled to the side and then headed back in the direction of the target. All this time we were diving at well over 300 knots.

'Just as the bend was coming into my gunsight picture, Doug called "Pull 'Bat', pull!" From the tone in his voice, I knew he was serious. He had been doing his job – monitoring the altitude during the dive while I concentrated on aiming at the target. I abandoned all thought of dropping bombs and began the pull out from the high-speed dive. We went below the flare parachute and the dark mountains on either side of the river. Finally, we began our climb back into the darkness. There was a sigh of relief, and a re-grouping of our thoughts as we set up for another delivery. By this time the cloud had moved away and we were able to put the bombs on target.

'At least one of the trucks must have been carrying fuel because we started a fire that lasted for about 20 minutes. On subsequent passes, we were able to get a couple more trucks carrying ammo. They began cooking off secondary explosions for the next half-hour, and were still exploding when we left the area.

'The DOOM Pussy patch has words that mean roughly "I have flown into the mouth of the cat from Hell". That is what it is like when you dive under flares and then return to the inky blackness of the night. I had a discussion with an F-100 pilot one afternoon about the value of a

second crew member. Doug and I were a team. We worked well together. I do not remember who won the argument, but the F-100 pilot flew a night mission the next evening and did not come back.'

During this time, everything was being learned on the job – tactics, weapons selection, bombing altitudes, even what survival gear should be carried. Most of the Canberra crews created their own homemade survival kits, each of which was personalised for the man carrying it. Navigator Maj 'Pappy' Boyington still had his survival kit 45 years after he left Vietnam;

'For openers, most of us carried a spare emergency radio beacon, an AN/URT-21. One was packed with the parachute, and if armed it could be rigged to switch "on" automatically by a lanyard pulling a plug when the parachute deployed. I carried a 0.38-cal Smith & Wesson Combat Masterpiece (short-barrel revolver) and extra ammo, a flare pen and flares, a switchblade knife with a hook blade for cutting shroud lines, a "Tropical First Aid Kit" type 2D/1, waterproof matches, "Survival Plant Recognition" study cards and an extra survival saw. I also carried a water bottle.'

All of this kit was stowed in a bag and pockets that hung down from a sort of garment that went around the waist. A separate leather gun belt with holster was worn slung down low from the waist like a 'Wild West' gunslinger, but in this case worn that way so as to keep it from fouling the ejection seat. In more modern aircraft like the F-4, in which crewmen wore a vest-like harness that clipped into the new Martin-Baker Mk VII seat and its built-in parachute, the sidearm was usually carried in a shoulder holster sewn onto the vest and harness.

Often, especially at night, a crew would be there one moment and gone the next, and no amount of clever kit could help them. For example, on the night of 10 February 1966 Capt Russell Palmer Hunter and his navigator Ernest Philip Kiefel, flying out of Da Nang in B-57B 52-1575, were working over targets in the *Steel Tiger* area of the Trail in southern Laos. The crew was operaring with a C-130 flare aircraft and had just attacked a target near Ban Vangthon. After making a second bombing pass on the target, Hunter radioed that there were problems with his jet and that he and Kiefel were ejecting. Observers reported a flash on the ground, and later the wreckage was located. However, no trace of either crewman was found.

As if the enemy were not threat enough, the 'Fool Killer' was always nearby with his club hoist casually over his shoulder, waiting for someone to show a lapse of attention, or to cut a corner in a safety-related checklist. Accidents and fiery death were always close by at the air bases, as the May 1965 tragedy at Bien Hoa graphically demonstrated. John DeCillo was an armourer – a group who proudly referred to themselves as 'B-57 Bummers' – who arrived at Da Nang as a young airman in September 1966. One potential disaster occurred on his first day at work as a member of one of the four-man arming crews on the Da Nang Canberra flightline;

'As I recall, the Crew Chief, Adam Kubiak of Buffalo, New York, got the load order and aircraft number at the arming shed. We proceeded out onto the ramp to start our work. Our entire crew except Adam were new guys in-theatre, and we were called "Jeeps" or "FNGs". As we were prepping our bomber for loading we got a call to drop whatever we were doing and race out to meet MSGT Roy Badge, the weapons squadron NCOIC (Non-Commissioned Officer In Charge) at the end of the runway. A Canberra was coming in with four hung napalm bombs on the wing pylons.

'I don't know what the other guys were thinking, but I thought, "I'm going to die today". By the time we got there the bomber had safely touched down and rolled to a stop, and emergency crews were on the scene. My job on the crew was to drive the MJ1 "Jammer" (a self-propelled bomb lift). The MJ1 is a rear-steering machine with hydraulic arms and an adjustable plate at the end. It is used for loading weapons of all types. A hard aluminium cradle on rollers is used on the plate end for handling napalm bombs.

'A hung bomb can be the result of several things. 1) The electric-powered rack malfunctioned and did not release the hooks holding the weapon. 2) The pylon chocks (sway braces) are tightened too much or are misaligned. 3) Pilot error. This particular SNAFU was caused by No 2. "Badger" motioned me to position the "Jammer" so that the first bomb was resting in the cradle. The other crew members were stationed to hold the weapon so as to keep it from rolling.

'These napalm bombs were 750-lb weapons with a six-pound charge of white phosphorous (WP) screwed into both ends. Normally, when the weapon was dropped two lanyards attached to the fuses on the WP charges were pulled out. This action allows a pin to shoot out and crack the casings of the WP charges. When the WP is exposed to air, it will ignite and can only be contained by depriving it of oxygen. In the case of the hung bombs, if one fell to the runway, the effect would be the same as if it were dropped in flight.

'With the cradle in place, the master sergeant grabbed the bomb by the fins, shook it and it dropped right into the cradle. I placed the bomb on the waiting Explosive Ordnance Disposal trailer. We repeated this routine three more times with the other hung bombs. Apparently, because of the flexible aluminium skin on the bombs, they had been chocked too tightly by another arming crew.'

Not every accident with bomb-laden aircraft had such a happy outcome at Da Nang. On 12 January 1966, pilot Capt Leon Boyd Smith and his navigator Maj Elijah Goar Tollett began their take-off roll with a full load of bombs. Observers on the ground noticed that the low-riding Canberra's nose was even closer to the tarmac than usual. Smith somehow managed to get the heavily laden aircraft just high enough to retract the undercarriage and B-57B 53-3876 seemed to struggle into the air. Before it reached the end of the runway, however, it settled back to earth and skewed around onto the infield. After it had come to a stop, Smith blew the canopy and the crew jumped over the side, with the pilot leaping out onto the wing.

Rescue workers raced toward the scene, but it appeared that the two crewmen would walk away from this one. Just as everyone was about to breathe again at the sight of the uninjured crew, one of the 500-lb bombs went off with an earth-shaking blast, cooking off the rest of the bomb load and reducing the aeroplane and its crew to dust. All that remained was a vast, muddy crater where the B-57 had sat.

THE DOOM PUSSY

The DOOM Pussy (DOOM being the acronym for Da Nang Officers' Open Mess) was a concept more than a mere shoulder patch, and a brotherhood of the kind that is forged in war and understood only by those who have been there. The patch itself was worn only by those men who had regularly flown into North Vietnam at night. On a shelf at the back of the horseshoe-shaped bar at the DOOM Club sat a stuffed black cat. The cat – like the famous Robin Hood Toby mug in the film *12 O'Clock High* – was turned to the wall when crews were on missions up north. When they returned, IF they returned, it was turned back to face forward and the liquor flowed freely.

Even before the B-57 units moved to Da Nang, a DOOM Pussy patch was proposed by, among others, 'Art' Jepson and Bob Galbreath;

'I designed the original patch. The plan was for it to say "Into the Mouth of the Cat of Doom" in English. Then one night at the bar in the compound at Bien Hoa, between rounds of "Diesel and Juice", a group of us including "Smash" Chandler, "Art" Jepson and some others started talking about maybe the motto should be in Latin because it would be more "classy". Then someone – my recollection is that it was "Art", though perhaps it was someone else – had the idea that it should be in Vietnamese. While I was looking for someone to translate the words the ramp explosion at Bien Hoa took place on 16 May 1965.

'"Art" was killed in the explosion, and that prompted me to move ahead with the patch because he had been so enthusiastic about it. We were living in the Dust Off barracks (occupied by Army "dust off" helicopter crews) at Tan Son Nhut after evacuating from Bien Hoa and, in desperation, I ended up asking one of the laundry girls there to translate the words. She translated it as "Trong Mieng Cua Con Men Cua Tham Phan". I took the design to the tailor shop in Saigon called Cheap Charlie's and ordered about 50 patches.'

The finished patch featured a cat with a patch over one eye, a crushed B-57 hanging from its mouth. Above it were the words 'The Canberra Night Fighters', for indeed that is what the crews considered themselves to be. After all, they were doing the same job, mostly involving dive-bombing and strafing, as fighter-bombers like the F-4, F-100 and F-105. While those jets did their jobs among the flak and SAMs in North Vietnam, only the B-57 squadrons regularly flew these missions at night.

The patch was a source of tremendous pride, with its combination of bravado and nihilism, and a dim view was taken of DOOM Pussy patches being owned by those who had not earned them. Soon, the DOOM Pussy became legendary, and inspired the title of two books by radio reporter Elaine Shepard about those early B-57 crews, along with a number of stories of the crews' adventures in and out of the aircraft whose veracity was at best dubious. The truth was hairy enough, however. The brotherhood of the DOOM Pussy was a small fraternity and the price of admission was often very, very high.

The coveted and legendary DOOM Pussy patch. The legend of the DOOM Pussy was born among a small group of the early Vietnam Canberra pilots and named for the Da Nang Officers' Open Mess. DOOM Pussy missions were those sorties flown over North Vietnam at night in an old aeroplane with no radar and no AAA or SAM warning apparatus. The legend, in phonetic Vietnamese, roughly translates to 'I have flown into the mouth of the cat and returned'. The more Western and less symbolic sentiment would translate to 'I have peered over the abyss at death'. Many who wore the patch, however, eventually did not return. The legend of the DOOM Pussy later inspired two books of that title by the war correspondent Elaine Shepard (*Bob Galbreath*)

Crewmen from the 8th BS wait outside their Da Nang barracks for the bus to take them to the flightline for the day's combat mission. Some have already donned their sidearms, while each wears a different expression ranging from thoughtful reflection to boredom (*Joe Rup*)

The original DOOM club at Da Nang, around which the legend of the DOOM Pussy was hatched. More than one journalist, unfamiliar with the US military's obsession with acronyms, wrongly interpreted the name as a reflection of the low morale and pessimism that supposedly permeated the ranks of US aviators. This early in the war, nothing could have been further from the truth (*William Boyington*)

Bob Galbreath distilled the psychology that went behind the patch and the concept of the DOOM Pussy. It was, as he points out, the work of nervous young men facing death almost nightly. Gung ho behaviour and displays of aerial machismo were things for the movies, but not for those who actually came face to face with their own mortality as a matter of course;

'I think the uniqueness of this patch lies in the fact that it was created very much with our mortality in mind, rather than the bravado and perceived invincibility which characterises most "blood and guts" military patches. It was created at a time when people were going north at night and disappearing. We didn't know why, and it was very scary.'

The stuffed cat behind the bar at the DOOM Club was faced backward more and more often as the two squadrons continued to play round-robin with their TDY tours. Those with wives and children back at Clark were in the strange situation of playing the role of husband and dad for two months and then, when the clock ran out, they were expected to go out and do their job, which was to be warriors and steely-eyed killers. The families were then in the position of wondering for the next 60 days if their husband or father would ever come home. Carol Rup, whose husband Joe was a navigator who flew with 8th BS, recalled;

'As far as being at Clark during the Vietnam War, it was one of the best assignments and in some ways, the worst. The best because I was a young wife and mum, and after being apart from Joe for ten months and being the sole caregiver to two young boys, I suddenly had the benefit of a live-in maid and baby-sitter, a yard boy and a "sew" girl!

'When the squadron was at Clark, it was a time of fun and socialising. There was plenty of stress, however, as we knew that our husbands would have to go back to the war. I guess the hardest thing was that we never knew who wasn't going to come home. Although we didn't have the advantage of the instant communications of today, we always heard through the

grapevine if there was an aircraft accident before any official word came down. Also, as a wife being on my own when he was in Vietnam, and doing things on my own, and being responsible for all the big decisions, it was a major readjustment when he returned. Looking back on the experience today, it was a good one and it made us stronger as a family. Of course, I can say that since we all returned unscathed.'

Meanwhile, the maintenance crews had no such close family contact. They worked constantly to keep the ageing bombers in the sky, fixing flak damage and broken parts due to the wear and tear of mounting combat hours on the airframes and engines. Unlike the new F-4s, which were being cranked out like model kits, the assembly line for the B-57 had shut down long ago. Only 250 bombers had been built by Martin, and even before they entered the war, the type had suffered ten years of wear, peacetime accidents and attrition. Pilot Robert 'Bat' Bateman recalled;

'Our maintenance crews did an excellent job keeping the jets ready to go on a 24-hour basis, seven days a week. There were no such things as weekends. Everyone just did his job, and a bit more, because this was a serious business. Nevertheless, there were problems, some large, some small, and some that worked themselves out in the strangest ways.

'On one mission, for example, the bulb for my gunsight went out. Had this been a training mission I would have gone back to base and landed. In Vietnam, this was not really an option. We had been flying at low level for some time, and there were bugs on the windscreen. On the first gunnery pass I noted that there was no gunsight, but in what appeared to be about the right place was a prominent bug. I fired a short burst of tracers to verify my suspicions. The tracers went where the bug pointed. We continued the mission, setting a large building on fire and causing a petroleum blaze that gave off plenty of smoke. Score one for the bugs!'

The DOOM Pussy continued to gobble men and aeroplanes, however, but on 17 April 1966 one crew got lucky. Or rather it is more accurate to say that the gutsy magicians and acrobats at the USAF Rescue and Recovery Service, with their HH-3 Jolly Green Giants and Air Commando A-1 Sandy escorts, created luck by the barrelful.

On this night, Capt Larry J Horacek (who had already survived an ejection eight months earlier) and his navigator, Capt D N Harnage, rolled in on an automatic weapons site on the North Vietnamese border with Laos, 25 miles north of the DMZ. The jet was on its second strafing run when it took several rounds from the ground and caught fire. Both men ejected and were quickly rescued by an HH-3. The incident was notable for two reasons. Firstly, it was the second time Horacek had survived being shot down in a Canberra, the first occasion being on 6 August 1965. And secondly, the aircraft, B-57C 53-3833, was the only 'two-stick' C-model to be shot down in the war.

LARRY AND JERE'S WILD RIDE

In mid-March 1966, patrolling FACs began to spot troops concentrating around a truck park on Route 9 in the *Tiger Hound* area of the Laotian Panhandle, specifically in the Xe Namkok River valley not far from Tchepone and its famously murderous flak guns. All kinds of tactical aircraft, FACs and observation aircraft were called into the area. On the morning of 15 March this included B-57s of the 8th BS. Among them was 'Yellowbird 22', crewed by pilot Capt Larry Mason and his navigator, Capt Jere Joyner. The latter had been rescued on 14 December 1965 after his B-57B (52-1565) had been shot down by AAA near Chu Prong mountain. Joyner had ejected, but his pilot, Capt Robert J Meroney, was still in the jet when it crashed and he was killed.

Flying 53-3906, they were carrying a heavy load – four 1000-lb bombs under the wings, seven 260-lb fragmentation bombs and six 500-lb GP bombs internally and 290 rounds of 20 mm ammunition for each of the guns. Mason and Joyner were flying on the wing of flight lead Capt Art Kono and his backseater, Capt Hank Shoughrin, in 'Yellowbird 21'.

After the crews had expended their bombs, they took turns making strafing runs under the direction of two FACs using the call signs 'Hound Dog 52' and 'Hound Dog 54'. Kono's guns stopped firing during one pass, and although he was near 'bingo' fuel and had only 800 rounds of 20 mm left, Mason decided to expend all of his ammunition before returning to base. The two jets were working down in a haze-filled valley, and were keeping close together to maintain visual contact. The FACs, flying O-1E Bird Dogs, came and went from view in the soupy mist.

After working over the truck park and a suspected troop concentration, the FAC found another target for Mason and Joyner. 'Our FAC, "Hound Dog 54", called us to come north a few miles from the village we had hit, where he had a disabled truck on the road', said Mason. When he began his strafing run, 'we would have been about one mile northwest of "Hound Dog 54" and about 1500 ft above the terrain in a river valley, with ridges on either side'.

What the FACs and bomber crews did not know was that this last target was a decoy truck – part of a flak trap. It was not a new trick, but even when vision was good it was not often easy to tell decoys from real trucks. The sky erupted with 37 mm and 57 mm flak from what was believed to be at least six guns. The first shell that hit 'Yellowbird 22' knocked it almost inverted before Mason could roll it upright again. The aircraft shook and the control column vibrated heavily in Mason's hands.

'I'm sure it was radar directed fire. The first one hit outside near the right wingtip and it just walked inward across the wing', Mason recalled.

He was wrestling with a jet that had been almost shot to pieces. A hole some 30 ft square had been opened up on the underside of the right wing, and it went all the way through to the uppersurface. One round had exploded at the root of the right flaps, which had been knocked down, and the nearby engine tailpipe was riddled with holes. Hydraulic fluid from burst lines sprayed against the hot engine and set it alight.

Mason fought for control of the violently shaking yoke, all the while trying to keep debris out of his eyes from the blast of wind blowing through a hole in the fuselage. Then the fire warning light came on. 'Hound Dog 54', having witnessed this and seeing the trail of flame in the jet's slipstream, broadcast, '"Yellowbird 22', look out!", then, "'Yellowbird 22', you're . . .' At that moment the guns of Tchepone hit the O-1E, sending it spiralling to the ground. 'Hound Dog 54' pilot Capt David H Holmes was killed. Minutes later a US Army OV-1A Mohawk appeared on the scene and was also downed. Its crew was never found.

Then, yet another round hit 'Yellowbird 22's' cockpit, entering through the lower right fuselage and exploding below and to the right of

The nose of B-57B 53-3906 of the 8th BS has been secured by a jack to ensure the nose gear does not collapse due to the heavy flak damage to the aircraft. Its pilot, Capt Larry Mason, flew the burning and badly shot-up aircraft back to Da Nang on 15 March 1966, thus saving the life of his backseater, Capt Jere Joyner, who was too severely wounded to survive an ejection. After the aircraft rolled to a stop and was foamed down, Mason signalled to the emergency crew to blow the 800-lb canopy, which could not be raised conventionally. He feared Joyner would bleed to death before the canopy could be cranked open manually. Note the large hole in the side of the cockpit from a 57 mm flak shell (*William Boyington*)

Joyner, knocking out electronics and cutting oxygen lines. The B-57 had lost all communications, including the intercom between Joyner and Mason, and almost all of the instruments had been rendered useless. They would have to eject.

As Mason looked for possible places to eject, Joyner passed forward a bloody note scrawled in pencil onto the back of a reconnaissance photograph. It read, 'Hit badly arm and leg. Losing blood'. Now Mason knew that ejection would quite possibly mean death for Joyner. He passed a tourniquet to his navigator and made up his mind to fly the battered jet back to Da Nang full of holes, the flaps on one side barely hanging on, and with no idea how much fuel was left. And as if that was not enough, as he got closer to base, he had an indication that the undercarriage was not functioning properly. Throughout the flight, Mason could see Joyner appearing and re-appearing in the rear view mirror as he sagged from weakness and then sat back up before going unconscious again.

They finally reached the shoreline of the South China Sea and turned south toward Da Nang. Mason began to let down for a straight-in approach, but his landing gear indicators showed two wheels partially down and the right main gear up and locked. Mason, for some reason, was waved off by the tower and had to make a single-engine go-around, which was difficult enough in a B-57 that was functioning well. When he finally came around again, a green flare was fired from an emergency vehicle, clearing him in. Mason, expecting to belly in, found to his relief that he was landing on three good wheels. The instruments were wrong. When they finally drew to a stop, Mason signalled to the emergency crew to blow the canopy – the quickest way to get to Joyner and give him aid.

Members of the various units on base, along with rescue workers, looked at the jet and shook their heads. How could this pile of junk have made it back and landed safely. There was a seven-foot by seven-foot hole in the right outer wing section and another large hole all the way through near the right wing root. And there were dozens of holes in the fuselage. The B-57 had lived up to its reputation for uncommon toughness.

Joyner, who had sustained 46 wounds from fragments, almost bled to death. Nevertheless, Mason later wrote to his wife, 'So help me, the guy actually grinned at me, and gave me a "thumbs up" signal'. Joyner went through a lengthy convalescent period.

For his heroism flying 'Yellowbird 22', Larry Mason was showered with awards, and became the only member of the Canberra

Capt William 'Pappy' Boyington examines the two holes on the outside of the rear cockpit of Mason and Joyner's 53-3906, where two shells entered and exploded. They left navigator Capt Jere Joyner with more than 40 shrapnel wounds from which he almost bled to death. After months of recovery, Joyner returned to the USAF. Mason was later awarded the Air Force Cross for valour, Joyner the Silver Star (*William Boyington*)

A B-57B heads inbound with a full load of napalm on the external pylons to what is probably a CAS mission. FACs were especially glad to have a flight of Canberras to work with due to their large internal and external weapons loads and long loiter time (*Robert Mikesh Archive*)

The outboard section of the right wing on B-57B 53-3906 was hit squarely by one of a barrage of radar-directed 57 mm flak rounds. After entering the wing the shell exploded, blowing the gun bays to pieces and throwing the skin outward. Even though the aircraft had been thoroughly holed, one engine was on fire and the instruments had been rendered useless, pilot Capt Larry Mason managed to fly the aircraft from Laos back to Da Nang and make a safe landing while his navigator was close to bleeding to death in the rear cockpit. Despite all the other damage, the wing was replaced with one from another aircraft and 53-3906 soldiered on, eventually being converted into a B-57G and serving as a testbed for the PAVE GAT programme (*William Boyington*)

community to be awarded the Air Force Cross, the USAF's highest medal for gallantry. Joyner received the Silver Star and eventually returned to duty in the US.

Meanwhile, Kono in 'Yellowbird 21', had been hit by the same flak trap and his B-57 caught fire. Luckily the blaze extinguished itself. Kono flew his holed aircraft back to Da Nang as well. After that, the 8th BS and other air assets returned and pounded the guns without let up. A VNAF A-1 was also shot down by the guns of Tchepone that day.

RIGHT INTO THE FIRE

Capt Joe Rup arrived at the wing HQ at Clark AFB in mid-1965. He would join the others in the 8th BS flying 60-day TDY tours, with 60 days back in the Philippines. After a while, this cycle became routine;

'I arrived in the Philippines about 0300 hrs one morning in early June 1965. My earliest recollection of the Philippines was that morning when I realised I had never seen bugs so big in my life. I was now at Clark AFB to train in the B-57 and go on to fly and fight in Vietnam.

'Within two weeks I had completed training and was on a transport to Da Nang to join the 8th BS. I was met at the aeroplane and taken to an old French barracks that housed the squadron aircrews. I was assigned a lower bunk just to the left inside the first floor entrance. That night after dinner, and a couple of beers at the DOOM club, we all went back to the barracks and turned in. I tried to go to sleep but it was tough that first night in the combat zone – the previous evening the base had been attacked and mortared by the VC.

'So I tossed and turned a bit and heard a strange sound I couldn't identify, and it seemed like all I could see in my mind's eye were those giant bugs I had left behind in the Philippines. I grabbed my flashlight and started to search for the origin of that sound. After checking under the bunk, in and around the lockers, I found the source in the top bunk. My bunk mate ground his teeth at night! When I found him, the other guys in our bay started laughing. They had stayed up just to have a joke at my expense. This was my introduction to the 8th and Da Nang.'

It was not long before Rup had become a veteran, flying missions over the trail and up North at night. On his third 60-day rotation, he brought his wife, Carol, and their children over. It came close to being the last they saw of him.

'During my third 60-day tour at Da Nang my wife and sons arrived in the Philippines. My commander allowed me to go to Clark to meet them and get them settled – then I had to return to finish the tour. Now I had already established a home for them and hired a full time house girl they would be comfortable with until I returned. I was home with them for three days as I now remember it, then I boarded a C-124 transport at Clark on the fourth morning at about 0600 hrs and arrived at Da Nang three hours later.

'One of the guys met me at the aircraft and drove me to the barracks. He asked if I'd like to fly that afternoon, and I immediately said yes. There was nothing more boring than sitting around all day without flying. But dummy that I was I didn't ask about the mission until I got to the barracks. Turns out that Ray Daeke, my pilot, and I were to be "Purple Seven" in an eight-ship attack on the Mu Gia pass in North Vietnam. It was unquestionably the most heavily defended pass in Vietnam. We took off at 1530 hrs, all jets departing uneventfully. It was only about an hour and ten minutes flying time to the pass.

'Led by our commander, Lt Col Dan Farr, we rolled in on the guns of Mu Gia one after the other, varying our roll-in headings, altitudes and exit headings. Still there was no way to avoid all the flak! By the time Ray and I rolled in I was already scared shitless. Large balls of fire were flying by the cockpit as I read off the altimeter so I could tell Ray when to unload our bombs on target. We did so and left the area on the deck, making our way to feet wet over the Tonkin Gulf and then south to Da Nang. The formation never did rejoin, but eventually we all made it back. Truthfully, this was probably one of the times I didn't think I would ever see my family again, and to think I had just brought them over to the Far East to join me.'

The merciless guns at Mu Gia Pass would claim scores more aircraft and dozens of aircrew until war's end. Rup would go on to survive 30 months in Vietnam and retire from the USAF a lieutenant colonel.

As this mission clearly showed, it was often just as dangerous to fly combat missions during the daytime as it was at night. While it was true that daytime combat in clear weather did not involve hidden obstacles like jagged mountains that were just waiting to 'swallow' an aeroplane, nor was the vertigo of night flying an issue, it was an inescapable fact that the Canberra had wings the size of barn doors, giving the jet a plan view that seemingly filled half the sky. Simply put, the B-57 was a fat target for enemy gunners. Worse, it was incapable of zipping around or escaping at supersonic speeds like the 'fast mover' F-4s, F-100s, F-105s and even F-104Cs that were then, oddly, being used for CAS. Still, the docile-looking B-57 was deceptively nimble, and capable of aerobatic moves that fighter pilots found hard to believe until they saw them. Still, once the gunners had the Canberra lined up it was difficult to get away.

On 6 October 1966 Capt G D Rippey and his navigator, Capt Louis Frank Makowski, of the 13th BS, were flying a day mission in B-57B 53-3888 just north of the DMZ near Kinh Mon. While awaiting their turn to roll in on the target they were hit by flak. With its tail on fire, the jet crashed within the DMZ. While Rippey was rescued by an HH-3E, rescue forces did not reach Makowski in time, and he spent the next six-and-a-half years as a prisoner of war in North Vietnam. 53-3888 had the distinction of being the first US jet to drop a bomb on Vietnam.

Only two days later another Canberra, this time from the 8th BS, was lost. B-57B 52-1512 (yet another aircraft requisitioned from the ANG to make up for attrition) of Capt R W Clark and navigator 1Lt P A

Viscasillas was hit by flak during a daylight interdiction raid. Clark tried to make it back to base, but the aircraft became uncontrollable and the crew ejected just before it crashed into the sea just off Da Nang. The two crewmen were picked up in good shape by a USAF HH-43 'Pedro'.

PATRICIA LYNN AND THE 'SPOOKS'

It is not quite accurate to say that the B-57Bs were the first tactical jets to be introduced to Vietnam. A variety of types such as the F-102 Delta Dagger interceptor and RF-101 Voodoo reconnaissance aircraft had been sent to the theatre in the two years before the 8th and 13th BSs arrived in August 1964. And even the B-57 courier aircraft from the latter units were not the first Canberras in Vietnam. That honour would go to the tiny detachment of top secret RB-57Es of Detachment 1 of the 33rd Tactical Group that flew under the code name *Patricia Lynn*. A year later they would receive their ultimate designation, Detachment 1, 6250th Combat Support Group (CSG), abbreviated to simply Det 1.

These first jets arrived in May 1963, and they would become some of the last US tactical aircraft to leave the country – the last Canberras to go departed South Vietnam eight years after the first one flew into Tan Son Nhut. During their time in country they operated under the tight veil of security that was usually reserved for the U-2 detachment, which also used the base.

The USAF had contracted with General Dynamics to modify a few B-57Es (called the 'Cadillac' of the Canberra family because of its modern 'amenities' and good flying characteristics). These aircraft were originally designed strictly for target towing, and they had a reel system built into them, as well as controls in the rear cockpit. They were later modified to act as ECM aggressor aircraft in the training of interceptor and other USAF crews in counter-ECM methods, serving in that capacity until the early 1980s.

General Dynamics was a logical choice to make modifications to the B-57Es, since it had carried out work on the long-winged RB-57Ds and was even then heavily modifying several Canberras into high-altitude reconnaissance aircraft 'stuffed' with the latest electronic spy equipment and known as the RB-57F (later WB-57F). The RB-57E was also equipped with optical reconnaissance gear, including the KA-1 36-inch focal length forward oblique camera and a panoramic K-56 camera as fitted to the U-2. These were mounted within a completely redesigned nose section that resembled an enormous black thimble.

The bomb-bay, which had housed the target cable reel system, was stripped and redesigned to carry reconnaissance gear. On the bomb-bay door – which was more like the pallet later used on the W/RB-57F – were mounted another KA-1 (this one vertical), a KA-477 split vertical day-night camera and infrared (IR) scanner and yet another KA-1, this one mounted obliquely to the left.

According to Robert Mikesh's account of the *Patricia Lynn* detachment's activities, so desperate was the need for any kind of tactical intelligence in Vietnam that on arrival at Tan Son Nhut the pilots and navigators that ferried the RB-57Es in were immediately turned into combat crews and briefed on missions by 2nd AD intelligence officers on the reconnaissance flights that they would make. The first mission was flown on 7 May 1963 (in 55-4243) by Capt Bill Scott and navigator Lt Bill Sung. Three days later, Capt Don Wachholz and navigator Lt Leo Otway completed their first mission (in 55-4245).

These sorties yielded results that had heretofore only been wished for, with the infrared imagery revealing VC training and base camps, small, hidden factories and storage dumps that crews flying over the area had previously been unable to locate from the air. From then on, the fleet of up to five *Patricia Lynn* aircraft operated literally round the clock from Tan Son Nhut. The third and fourth aircraft to be added were 55-4237 and 55-4249 and, finally, on 22 November 1965 RB-57E 55-4264 arrived from the factory in the all-matt black finish that would soon be the trademark of the five aircraft of Det 1. The earlier aircraft also had their Air Defence Command grey finish replaced with matt black. The RB-57Es would be known by their call sign, 'Moonglow'.

Considering the frantic pace demanded of Det 1, and the dangerous nature of their mission, it is surprising that all of the *Patricia Lynn* aircraft were not lost to attrition during their eight years in combat. As it was, they suffered their fair share of casualties in Vietnam, yet it was more than two years before Det 1 lost its first aeroplane. On 5 August 1965, while on a night IR reconnaissance mission, Capt Richard E Damon and backseater Capt Richard C Crist in 55-4243 were hit by small arms fire, forcing them to head back to base. However, the aircraft began to burn in the bomb-bay and observers saw flames streaming from the Canberra's belly. Finally, the two airmen had to eject about 1.5 miles short of the Tan Son Nhut runway and were safely recovered.

It would be more than three years before Det 1 lost another jet. This time, on 21 October 1968, Maj J W Johnston and navigator Maj P N Walker were making reconnaissance passes over VC positions three miles southeast of Truc Giang, in the Mekong Delta, when 55-4264 was hit by small arms fire. In order to get the best sensor returns, the aircraft was flying straight and level at 2000 ft at the time it was hit, knocking out the right engine and causing it to burst into flames. The crew ejected with minor injuries and were recovered.

Oddly, although it is believed that most of the highly classified *Patricia Lynn* sorties were flown over Laos and the Ho Chi Minh Trail, and in some cases Cambodia, both losses were suffered over South Vietnam. At least one B-57E was reconfigured by General Dynamics to replace these combat losses.

An RB-57E from the highly secret Detachment 1 *Patricia Lynn* programme. These aircraft were taken from the stock of B-57E target tugs and fitted with a suite of reconnaissance cameras and the latest infrared photography and mapping equipment. Note the unusual nose fitted to the aircraft. This photograph was taken at the *Patricia Lynn* ramp at Tan Son Nhut. The fuselage marking below the cockpit is the Det 1 insignia (*USAF*)

RB-57E 55-4264 is seen here parked safely within a recently erected hardened revetment at Tan Son Nhut AB in 1966. The highly secret *Patricia Lynn* programme, with only six jets modified to that specification, set up shop at the airfield in May 1963. Planned as a temporary programme, Det 1 operated uninterrupted for more than eight years. It was the first unit to deploy infrared reconnaissance equipment to the battlefield, hence the tightened security around the aircraft. 55-4264 fell to flak on 21 October 1968 (*USAF*)

B-57B 53-3860 was one of the aircraft used in the *Tropic Moon II* programme, which tested systems that would ultimately be incorporated into the B-57G. In fact the aircraft was later converted into a B-57G and returned to Southeast Asia with the 13th BS for another tour in this configuration (*Robert Mikesh Archive*)

Over the period of *Patricia Lynn*, all manner of new sensor equipment was tried out. In fact the original programme, which was meant to test the IR sensor equipment under battlefield conditions, was only scheduled to last several months at the most. Eight years later, the state-of-the-art had advanced dramatically, and there were plenty more new gadgets to be tried out.

THE VNAF EXPERIMENT

Both during and after the conflict, the VNAF's B-57s have been quite visible whenever the subject of the Canberra's role in the Vietnam War is discussed. However, the VNAF flew the aircraft operationally for only about seven months. While a few B-57B/Cs were marked up in VNAF colours and flown by Vietnamese pilots (though as often as not with a USAF pilot or navigator in the back seat), the aircraft were always under the control of the 8th or 13th BSs.

The aircraft bearing VNAF markings were parked on the B-57 flightline at Da Nang. When one went down for periodic maintenance, another Canberra would have its USAF markings stripped and South Vietnamese insignia applied so that the same number of VNAF bombers would always remain visible for the eyes of North Vietnamese spies, of whom there was no shortage, and ostensibly for the benefit of the South Vietnamese people's morale.

The South Vietnamese government began pressuring the Johnson administration to provide them with jets to supplement their A-1 Skyraiders almost as soon as the first Canberras arrived at Clark AFB in the spring of 1964. The US government finally gave in, since they could not argue with the fact that other allied nations in the region such as South Korea and Taiwan had been provided with American jets for the better part of a decade by then. So, by August 1965, Saigon newspapers were boldly proclaiming that the VNAF was soon to be flying jet bombers. In fact the training of pilots had already started more than a year earlier in relative secrecy.

Lt Col Don Nation was put in charge of the training, writing the syllabus for the VNAF pilots;

'I set up a Phase I training programme for VNAF pilots, six to start with, then later it became a fully fledged B-57 Phase I and II Combat Training Program for VNAF pilots and navigators, and we also trained the groundcrews. I was VNAF Commander-in-Chief Gen Nguyen Cao

49

Ky's personal B-57 instructor pilot, which continued even after he became the prime minister.'

The first VNAF pilots got their preliminary training at Clark AFB in May 1964, shortly after the 8th and 13th BSs arrived there. The training programme was controlled by the 2nd AD, which acted as liaison with the South Vietnamese government. The first three students all wore patches indicating that they had at least 500 combat missions behind them. More importantly, they had some previous jet training in T-33s, which helped considerably. The most difficult adjustment in the transition from propeller aeroplanes such as the A-1 to jets is getting used to how much faster everything takes place, from getting the landing gear up on time, to how fast the runway comes up on landing. The student, at least at first, is almost always 'behind' the aeroplane.

Nation considered this first batch of B-57 students to be outstanding pilots, especially good at bomb delivery and strafing. The next group of three, who would be trained at Tan Son Nhut, included future South Vietnamese Premier Ky, Col Luan and Maj Van, the latter two both holding important positions within the VNAF. Ky famously took Nation and some of the other US officers in the training programme on a nocturnal tiger hunt on elephant-back in the Central Highlands of Vietnam. No tigers were encountered, but they did bag two deer.

At last, on 9 August 1965, a formal presentation ceremony of the Canberras was arranged for members of the South Vietnamese government and other VIPs at Tan Son Nhut. Already, three dual-control B-57Cs had been brought over from Clark so that Ky, who was now Premier following a coup, and still commander of the VNAF, as well as Capts Toung and Long, could refamiliarise themselves with the B-57. These aircraft were adorned with VNAF insignia for the occasion, with the removed USAF markings leaving conspicuous shiny patches on the aluminium skin of the aircraft.

According to Bob Mikesh's account, the grandstands groaned under the weight of South Vietnamese and Southeast Asian Treaty Organisation 'brass' and diplomatic 'bigwigs' present for the ceremony. The B-57s, which had already taken off and were orbiting 'offstage' as the stands filled up, now thundered by in a high-speed, low altitude pass for the assembled VIPs. What was not publicised was that the aircraft, at least during some critical phases of flight, were under the control of USAF pilots who were flying in the back seat. Nation was flying with Ky who, while a more than competent pilot, had not taken part in the rehearsal for the show, so Nation took over for the landing, which he performed with special flourishes.

As the aircraft rolled out to the end of the runway, the US pilots slid down into the cockpit from the back seats and the VNAF pilots taxied back to the reviewing stand 'solo'. Ky, as usual, wore his dashing, custom-fitted black flight suit with a lilac-coloured silk scarf (his beautiful and charming wife, Madame Mei, had a matching suit and scarf). To his credit, Ky made sure the US pilots were invited to the champagne reception that followed the presentation of the aircraft. For a while after this Ky made sure that 'his' B-57s were conspicuous no matter where they were in Vietnam, and three or four were always parked on the ramp at Da Nang for the length of the 'experiment'.

Air Commodore Nguyen Cao Ky, commander-in-chief of the VNAF (and soon to be Prime Minister of South Vietnam), climbs down from a B-57C while his personal instructor pilot, Capt Don Nation, waits in the back seat. Ky was amongst a handful of Vietnamese pilots who became proficient in the Canberra, but a programme to equip the VNAF with the bombers fell apart after less than a year. While some of the VNAF personnel who had previous jet trainer experience soon got to grips with flying the jet bomber, most did not. They were used to the propeller-driven A-1 Skyraider which, while by no means a 'soft' aircraft to fly, did not demand such quick reactions as a jet. A few unfortunate accidents discouraged the VNAF students even further (*Don Nation*)

B-57B 52-1530, seen here on the Da Nang flightline, was a recently-arrived ANG jet whose insignia had been stripped from the tail and replaced with VNAF markings. The VNAF's B-57 programme was very much a product of politicians. With only a small handful of trained pilots, it usually consisted of little more than a few 8th and 13th BS aircraft with their USAF markings temporarily changed to VNAF livery and parked so that they could easily be seen by the local civilians and the VC (*via John DeCillo*)

Not all the VNAF pilots were 'gun shy' around the B-57, and some flew combat missions with US pilots in the back seat. Here, a VNAF pilot prepares to embark on a mission in 52-1551 with his US instructor in the back seat. Significantly, this is a B-57B, and it does not have controls in the rear cockpit. Of note on this aircraft is the black bomb-bay door and the red kangaroo 'tagged' on the aircraft by mischievous RAAF personnel, who put their mark on many 8th and 13th BS B-57s (*USAF*)

The trained VNAF pilots flew missions from Da Nang with both squadrons, and with a USAF crewman aboard, until they were ready to fly with the American units using all-Vietnamese crews. On one occasion, an all-VNAF flight flew a strike mission against the VC and then went thundering down the major thoroughfare of Saigon at 300 ft AGL! It was a propaganda coup, but over at Clark things had begun to deteriorate with the next group of four pilots and two navigators. A few close calls and a freak accident devastated their confidence. On top of that, the B-57B/C was a simple, no-frills aeroplane, meaning it had no control boost or hydraulic aids to make manoeuvring easier. It simply had to be manhandled about the sky. This made it difficult for the slightly built Vietnamese airmen.

The new students began to report in sick on scheduled flying days, and an accident at Naval Air Station Cubi Point, in the Philippines, involving Lt Lom and his USAF instructor resulted in a B-57 being written off, although the crew escaped unscathed. However, the incident that many believe put paid to the programme happened on 23 February 1966 when B-57B 52-1512, flown by an all-Vietnamese crew led by Maj N N Bien, diverted to Pleiku with hung bombs and low fuel during a strike mission. The aircraft was successfully de-armed, but Maj Bien was unable to start the engines to taxi the aircraft back to the parking ramp – the inexperienced VNAF groundcrew had failed to install the starter cartridges correctly. They decided to push the aircraft by hand, with Bien staying aboard to steer using differential braking, as the B-57B had no nose-wheel steering.

With insufficient hydraulic pressure to brake, the jet began to roll down a slight hill, becoming uncontrollable and veering off the taxiway. Bien, who was a highly respected aviator and one of the spearheads of the B-57 programme, leapt from the aircraft, but fell and was run over by the left main wheel. He was fatally injured. This freak accident devastated the already demoralised student pilots.

After this, the VNAF B-57 programme simply withered and died, and on 20 April 1966 it was officially terminated. One of the USAF instructor pilots involved in the operation commented many years later that 'it was not that the Vietnamese were incapable of flying the aeroplane, but rather that they were rushed into it by their leaders. Not given ample training time or flying hours, they were ultimately unable to raise anything more than a token force that was not up to combat fitness'.

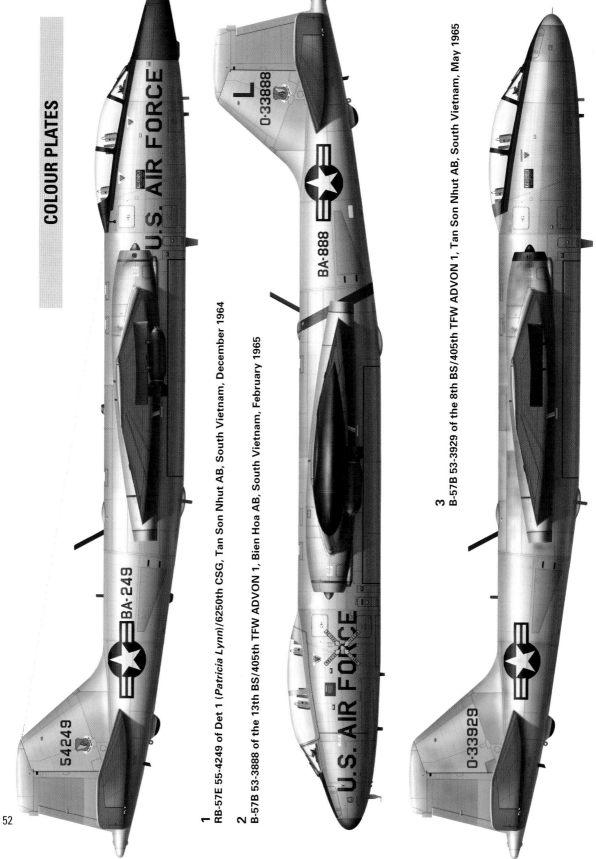

1
RB-57E 55-4249 of Det 1 (*Patricia Lynn*)/6250th CSG, Tan Son Nhut AB, South Vietnam, December 1964

2
B-57B 53-3888 of the 13th BS/405th TFW ADVON 1, Bien Hoa AB, South Vietnam, February 1965

3
B-57B 53-3929 of the 8th BS/405th TFW ADVON 1, Tan Son Nhut AB, South Vietnam, May 1965

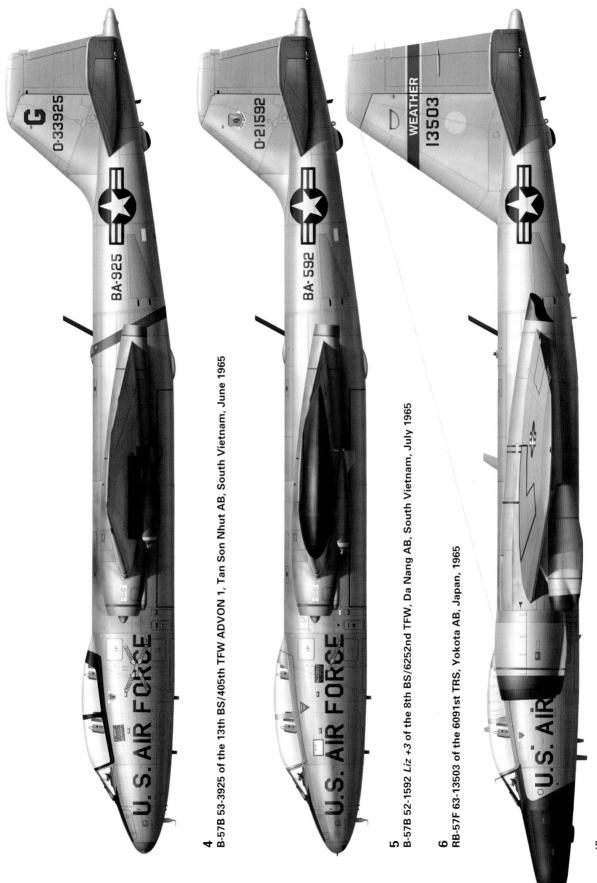

4
B-57B 53-3925 of the 13th BS/405th TFW ADVON 1, Tan Son Nhut AB, South Vietnam, June 1965

5
B-57B 52-1592 *Liz +3* of the 8th BS/6252nd TFW, Da Nang AB, South Vietnam, July 1965

6
RB-57F 63-13503 of the 6091st TRS, Yokota AB, Japan, 1965

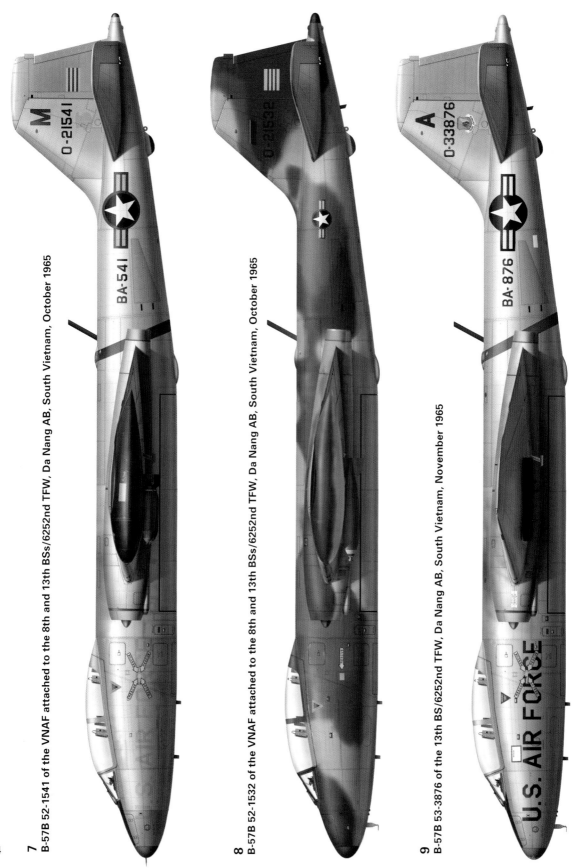

7
B-57B 52-1541 of the VNAF attached to the 8th and 13th BSs/6252nd TFW, Da Nang AB, South Vietnam, October 1965

8
B-57B 52-1532 of the VNAF attached to the 8th and 13th BSs/6252nd TFW, Da Nang AB, South Vietnam, October 1965

9
B-57B 53-3876 of the 13th BS/6252nd TFW, Da Nang AB, South Vietnam, November 1965

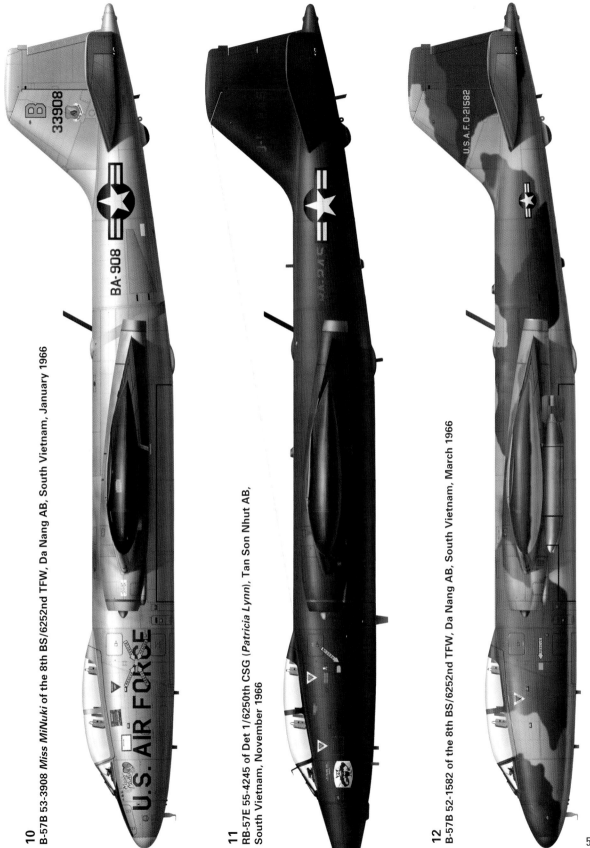

10
B-57B 53-3908 *Miss MiNuki* of the 8th BS/6252nd TFW, Da Nang AB, South Vietnam, January 1966

11
RB-57E 55-4245 of Det 1/6250th CSG (*Patricia Lynn*), Tan Son Nhut AB, South Vietnam, November 1966

12
B-57B 52-1582 of the 8th BS/6252nd TFW, Da Nang AB, South Vietnam, March 1966

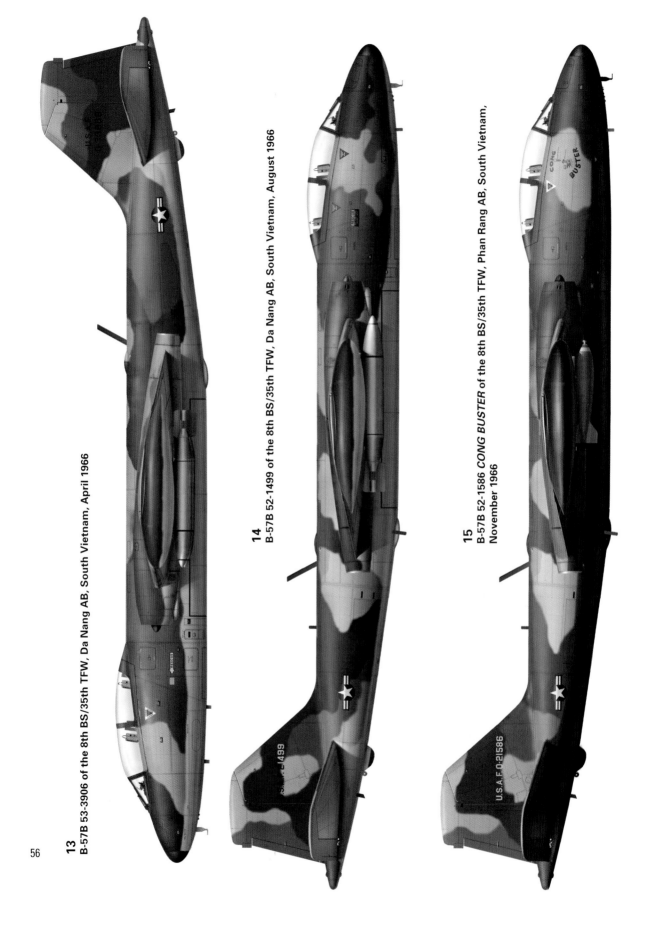

56

13
B-57B 53-3906 of the 8th BS/35th TFW, Da Nang AB, South Vietnam, April 1966

14
B-57B 52-1499 of the 8th BS/35th TFW, Da Nang AB, South Vietnam, August 1966

15
B-57B 52-1586 *CONG BUSTER* of the 8th BS/35th TFW, Phan Rang AB, South Vietnam, November 1966

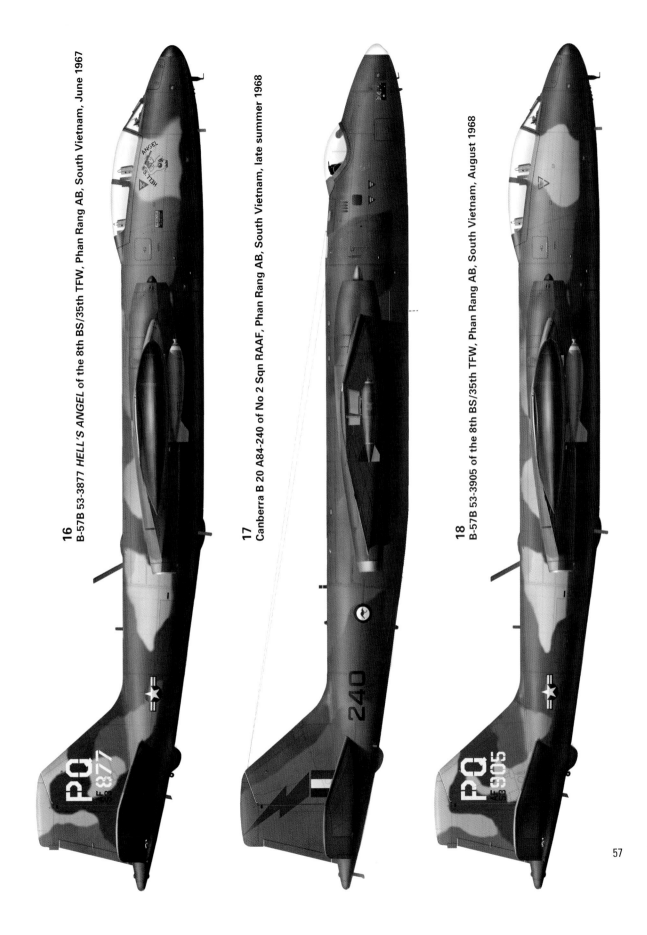

16
B-57B 53-3877 *HELL'S ANGEL* of the 8th BS/35th TFW, Phan Rang AB, South Vietnam, June 1967

17
Canberra B 20 A84-240 of No 2 Sqn RAAF, Phan Rang AB, South Vietnam, late summer 1968

18
B-57B 53-3905 of the 8th BS/35th TFW, Phan Rang AB, South Vietnam, August 1968

57

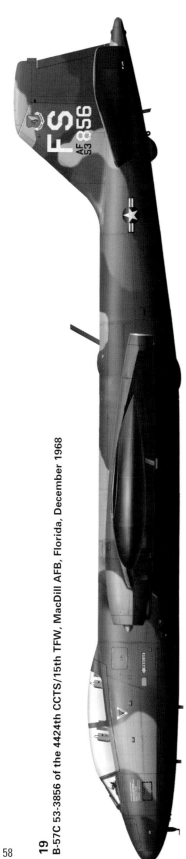

19
B-57C 53-3856 of the 4424th CCTS/15th TFW, MacDill AFB, Florida, December 1968

20
B-57B 52-1567 of the 8th BS/35th TFW, Phan Rang AB, South Vietnam, March 1969

21
B-57B 52-1551 of the 8th BS/35th TFW, Phan Rang AB, South Vietnam, October 1969

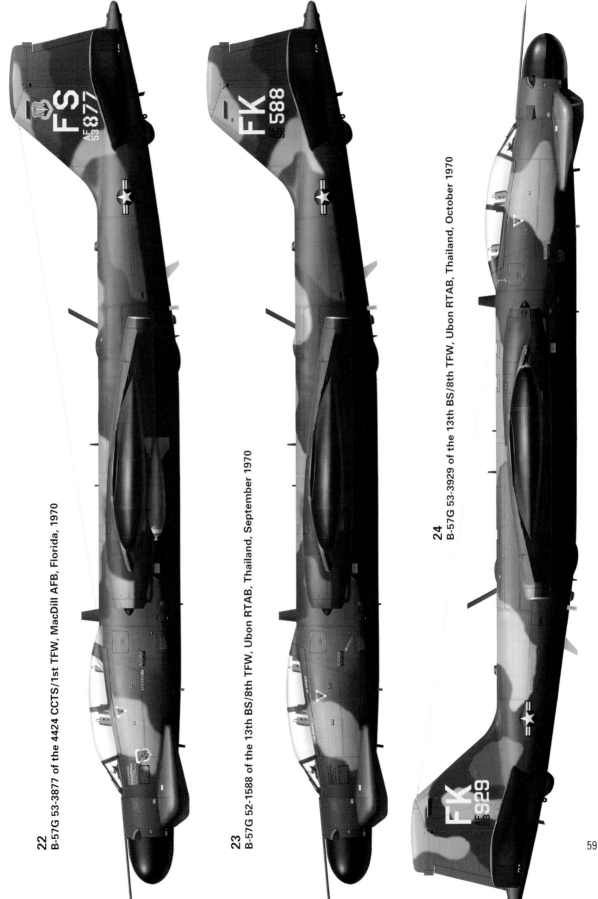

22
B-57G 53-3877 of the 4424 CCTS/1st TFW, MacDill AFB, Florida, 1970

23
B-57G 52-1588 of the 13th BS/8th TFW, Ubon RTAB, Thailand, September 1970

24
B-57G 53-3929 of the 13th BS/8th TFW, Ubon RTAB, Thailand, October 1970

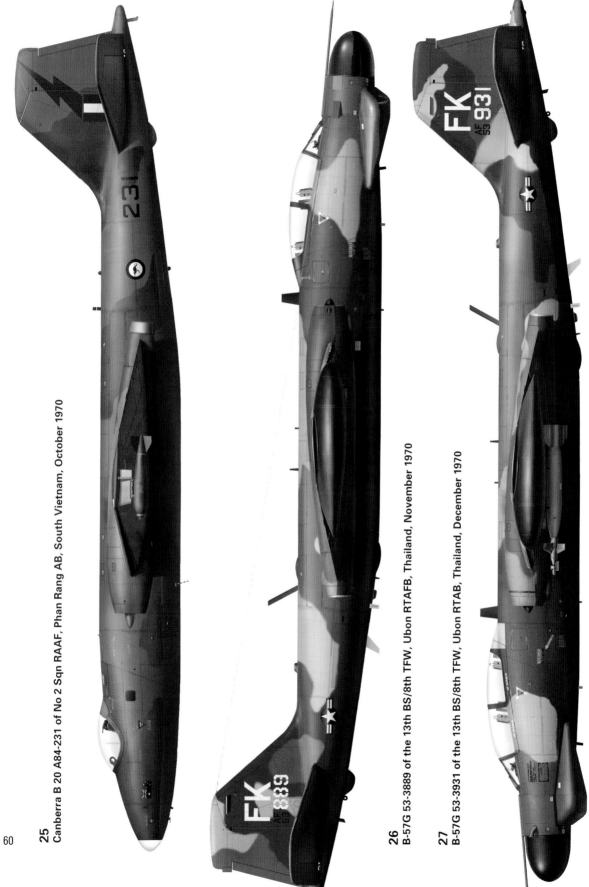

25
Canberra B 20 A84-231 of No 2 Sqn RAAF, Phan Rang AB, South Vietnam, October 1970

26
B-57G 53-3889 of the 13th BS/8th TFW, Ubon RTAFB, Thailand, November 1970

27
B-57G 53-3931 of the 13th BS/8th TFW, Ubon RTAB, Thailand, December 1970

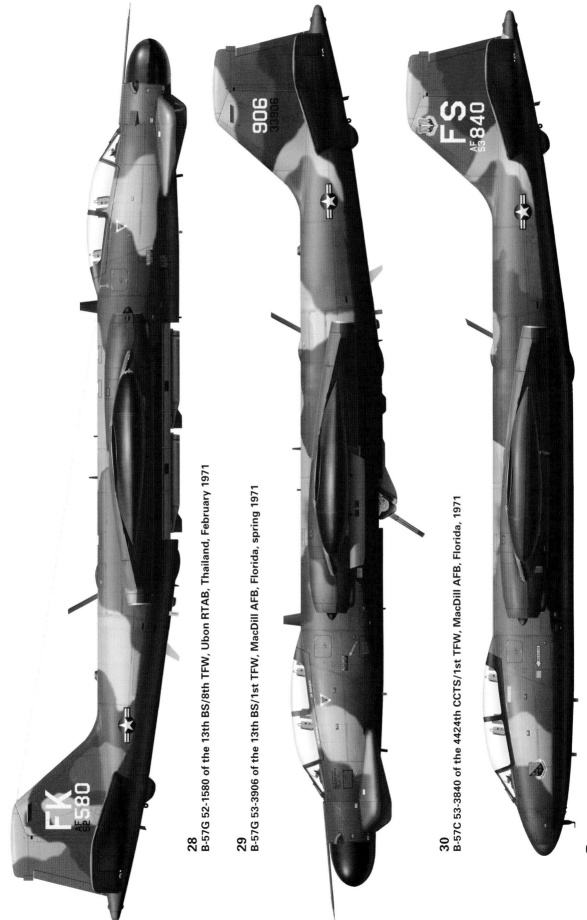

28
B-57G 52-1580 of the 13th BS/8th TFW, Ubon RTAB, Thailand, February 1971

29
B-57G 53-3906 of the 13th BS/1st TFW, MacDill AFB, Florida, spring 1971

30
B-57C 53-3840 of the 4424th CCTS/1st TFW, MacDill AFB, Florida, 1971

PHAN RANG

D a Nang was, by 1967, probably the busiest one-runway airfield in the world. The base itself was bursting at the seams, with each branch of the service operating from there, up to and including the US Coast Guard. To the south, on the coast, a brand new base had been under construction near the town of Phan Rang. When it was decided to replace the F-100s at Da Nang with F-4 Phantom IIs, the Canberras, which also came under the control of the same 35th TFW as the Super Sabres, moved to the new base along with the 'Huns'.

For the first time in their almost three years in Vietnam the 8th and 13th BSs finally had enough room from which to operate effectively, and their jets were at last provided with the protection of revetments. Crews described that the setting at Phan Rang was 'beautiful', with a view of the mountains on one side and the blue South China Sea on the other.

Maj Bill Maxson was able to get himself out of a safe staff job in the Pentagon and directly into combat at this time. He quickly went through B-57 training at Hill AFB, Utah, and then on to Clark for further and more realistic combat training, before reaching Phan Rang on a three-month TDY rotation. Maxson, who had flown many of the aircraft in the USAF inventory by that time, did not have experience in the Canberra. However,

By the summer of 1967, the USAF had gotten its priorities correct, and long before the base at Phan Rang was finished sturdy revetments for each aircraft were constructed. In this aerial view, the B-57 parking area can be seen to the left, while the revetments to the right are filled with F-100D Super Sabre fighter-bombers (*USAF*)

'the B-57 was an easy aircraft to learn about and to fly. It had two very reliable engines and was "honest" in its flying characteristics'. The B-57's one deadly flying characteristic was its poor engine-out performance. When one J65 was lost the pilot had to react quickly to the sudden yaw and roll into the dead engine. Power had to be applied slowly to the remaining good engine, so missed-approach go-arounds on one engine were treacherous and often fatal.

Maxson and the other 'FNGs' had to learn dive-bombing, 'skip' bombing, strafing and 'swooping'.

Among the new crop of aircrew who arrived with Maxson was Lt Col Benjamin L 'Bennie' Davis, who later rose to the rank of four-star general. Davis became the 13th BS's Operations Officer. The 405th TFW's wing commander at Clark AFB at this time was none other than Col Charles 'Chuck' Yeager, who flew his own stripped-down, heavily waxed Canberra with the tip tanks removed and the external fuel carried in the bomb-bay to decrease drag and make the aeroplane faster. Yeager, according to some of his pilots, flew combat missions, although 'off the record' because he was not combat qualified in the Canberra. He also used his 'hot rod' B-57 to visit the units in his widely scattered command.

'In the beginning', said Maxson, 'we flew two-ship, daytime, in-country missions with our newly assigned navigators. As new pilots, we were generally assigned experienced backseaters to help us learn the ropes and keep us out of trouble. These day missions were flown in I, II, III and IV Corps, mostly in support of ground troops. Vietnam was divided up into four corps stretching 1000 miles from the low lands in the Mekong Delta to the south up to the rugged, white karst highlands in the north.

'By now I was entering the "big leagues" of combat flying. The squadron would typically fly a stream of B-57s from sundown to sunup. Take-offs were spaced about 50 minutes apart all night long, every night of the week. The single-ship B-57 would "coast out" or go "feet wet" near Cam Ranh Bay, just north of Phan Rang, after flying through a threat area off the end of the runway (where the VC would fire on departing and landing aircraft), which was protected by "Puff" – AC-47 gunships that suppressed enemy anti-aircraft guns.

'After climbing north to 30,000 ft over the South China Sea, the single B-57s would turn west near Da Nang and head for Laos, and their secret war over the Ho Chi Minh Trail. All night trucks travelled these jungle "highways" with headlights on, but muted to hide their movements.

'We were briefed that the trucks were made in Czechoslovakia, specially designed for traversing the rugged terrain, even crossing shallow rivers and sandbars. They were driven empty to the borders of North Vietnam, where they were loaded up and sent south down the Trail. We got to look at one of these trucks close up at Nakhon Phanom RTAB after it was captured intact along the Trail.'

B-57B 53-3928 of the 8th BS drops a load of M117 750-lb bombs through the undercast far below during a *Combat Sky Spot* mission. This radar bombing technique, in which the flight dropped on the signal of a pathfinder aircraft, was not popular with many of the US crews. However, RAAF Canberras achieved considerable accuracy with this method of bombing (*Robert Mikesh Archive*)

These trucks, which the B-57 crews spent so much blood and treasure destroying, were really quite remarkable recalled Maxson;

'In addition to being very well built structurally, they had an inflation system to soften or harden the tyres depending on the soil conditions. The vehicle I saw at Nakhon Phanom AB was like a US four-ton truck. They were difficult targets, running along at night hiding from us however they could.'

There was much debate – both at the time, and after the war – about the prudence and tactical value of putting multi-million-dollar aircraft and irreplaceable pilots at such peril to destroy $4000 trucks and their cargo. However, it was not the aircrews' place to debate such things, but rather to destroy as many trucks as they could, just as they were ordered to do. They even had an unofficial organisation known as the 'Centurion Club', which was open only to those crews who had at least 100 confirmed truck kills. Some had double and triple that number.

By the time the B-57s had arrived at Phan Rang, tactics for going after the Trail traffic at night had been honed to a fine art. After being vectored to the general area of the hunting ground along the trail using VOR (VHF omnidirectional radio ranging), the B-57s would check in with the nearest FAC, who by this stage in the war had the most sophisticated night-vision equipment available at the time.

'Those night FACs were the bravest of souls!' said Maxson. 'Flying around in extremely rugged terrain, through mountain passes, they would somehow evade enemy ground fire and locate trucks for us'.

When a target was located, the B-57s would be requested to descend from higher altitude down to their 'perch' altitude (6000 ft AGL) and to begin their attack. Being jets, the B-57s, even with their large fuel capacity, had to remain as high as they could for as long as possible so as to conserve fuel in the thinner air. As they descended, fuel consumption went up rapidly. The target marked, the B-57 would begin its dive-bombing run and the crew would go through its checklist for this. Firstly, they went to 100 percent oxygen to improve their night vision. Secondly, they turned off all navigation and running lights so as to make it more difficult for the gunners to see them. Thirdly, both men hooked up the zero-delay lanyard on their ejection seats so that their parachutes would open immediately in case of a low altitude bailout, even if they were incapacitated.

'A moonlit night with a light haze made our silhouette more visible to gunners, so we prayed there was no "gunner's moon"', recalled Maxson.

The FACs dropped what were known as 'log markers' that burned brightly when they hit the ground. Then the FAC would instruct the bomber to aim for a spot so many metres away and in a particular direction from the log marker. The same technique was used with smoke rockets during the daytime.

The crew of B-57B *THE MAFIA* wait for a groundcrewman to finish his last-minute duties before taxiing out on a combat mission from Phan Rang in 1967. Nose art on USAF Canberras when it appeared at all tended to be simple, and was usually applied with felt-tip markers (*Joe English*)

'We were always aware that the enemy was more than likely eavesdropping on our frequency, so instead of giving compass directions for our run-in heading, the FAC would say "from Atlanta to Miami" instead of north to south', Maxson explained. 'When cleared in "hot", throttles went to idle, speed boards were out and we would roll into the dive and then roll out on the correct heading to the target. We would aim at the target and release bombs at about 3000 ft.

'On the way down the dive, we often encountered AAA fire – 37 mm flak guns were commonplace on the trail. About every fourth round was a tracer, so you could get some idea of how well the gunner was tracking you. Crews likened these 37 mm tracers to red hot beer cans.'

And so the missions would go. After completing the dive and weapons delivery, if they were lucky enough to avoid the flak, the crew would climb back up to their 'perch' altitude and wait for instructions from the FAC for the next drop.

During this time, the B-57s remained the only aircraft in theatre to use the M35 and M36 incendiary cluster bombs, or as they were universally known, 'funny bombs'. During night missions, the aircraft usually carried two 750-lb general purpose bombs under each wing, while four of the 'funny bombs' would fit in the bomb-bay.

'Of course, even though we flew hundreds of these missions, certain ones stand out', said Maxson. 'Like the night I, along with substitute back-seater Willie Richardson, destroyed eight trucks – an unusual number for one sortie. We had a lot of flak, but had stopped a convoy on one of our passes. Once stopped, picking off the trucks in the convoy was much easier. Other strike aircraft following us were quick to press the advantage. We also had a serious problem with fuel. One of the external tanks wouldn't transfer its contents, so we were flying an aircraft that was quite difficult to maintain lateral control in. We decided to divert to Nakhon Phanom, and made it safely.'

For this mission, Maxson was awarded the Silver Star and Richardson the Distinguished Flying Cross.

THE RELUCTANT BACK-SEATER

Ed Rider was a Canberra pilot who had come up through the enlisted ranks, having done a stint as an Airborne Electronics Technician on the B-57 in the late 1950s. Ten years later he was a captain flying the Canberra out of Phan Rang. Rider was known for his aggressive flying and his own particular tactics that were more suited to a nimble fighter-bomber than the big B-57. And by Rider's own admission, 'there were only about two navigators left who would fly with me'. Before the war was all over he had completed more than 400 combat missions. The following is Rider's account of one such mission in 1968;

'The "Yellowbirds" were back at Phan Rang flying night interdiction missions in the southern part of North Vietnam and along the supply routes down through Laos. I had a patch on my party flight suit that said "Laotian Highway Patrol".

'Other than the two navigators in the squadron who would willingly fly with me, the others did not like my highly unorthodox tactics. I tried to point out to them that other pilots were getting shot up – or shot down – while I never took hits and killed more trucks than most. Those idiots were coming back with their aeroplanes full of holes and getting medals for it. Anyway, my navigator came down with a bad case of "Ho's Revenge" and the other navigator was already flying, so someone had to be volunteered. The hand of fate laid its clammy finger on Bill. After an earlier adventure that ended in a belly landing due to hydraulic failure, he had sworn never to fly with me again. We had to drag him scratching and spitting, so to speak, to the aeroplane.

'We were taking off at midnight to hit a truck park way up in Laos. I asked the crew chief if his aeroplane was ready, and when he said yes I gave him four beers to put into the rear compartment and told him to button it up (close all inspection doors). I didn't insult him by inspecting the jet. The crew chiefs liked for me to fly their aeroplanes and I never had one let me down. I went around with the armourer and checked the fuses on the bombs for proper settings and the arming wires for proper routing. Then I spread my maps on the ramp and showed the crew chief and armourer where we were going and what we were supposed to hit.

'We were in the northeast monsoon season and had 40 knots of wind blowing down the runway. The standard night departure called for a right turn to the south after take-off until reaching the coast, then a turn to the east and then follow the coast to Cam Ranh Bay and turn on course. This was supposed to keep you out of the outgoing artillery, but it wasted about 3000 lbs of fuel, so naturally I didn't follow it. After I raised the gear I turned off all external lights so that the air traffic controllers in the tower could not see me. When I was high enough to drop a wing, I turned right 270 degrees so as to cross the west end of the runway headed northwest. I roared across the 101st Airborne encampment and shook all the grunts out of bed and then headed up the valley that led to Dalat in the mountains. The hills on either side

B-57B 53-3898, a veteran of the 8th BS since the unit's nuclear alert days in Korea, is readied for a night mission at Phan Rang. The large door that swung down from the lower wing was for servicing and arming the two 20 mm cannon. One oddity about this photograph is the 2.75-inch rocket pod mounted under the left wing. B-57 crews very rarely used these, and most did not consider them to be reliable weapons. 53-3898 was later converted into a B-57G and sent back into combat in 1970 with the 13th BS (*John DeCillo*)

Armourer Sgt James Logan fuses a load of 500-lb Mk 82 bombs at Phan Rang in 1967. The B-57s more commonly carried older, box-fin bombs internally and 750-lb bombs under the wings. These modern aerodynamic bombs did not fit in the Canberra's bomb-bay very well (*John DeCillo*)

were invisible as there were no lights on the ground, but if I maintained the proper heading I would not run into any rocks before I got high enough to clear them. Bill was somewhat unhappy with this exercise. In due course we climbed out of the valley and turned north to Pleiku, and points north.'

'We checked in with "Blind Bat", our C-130 "flare ship", and from more than 50 miles out we could see his flares and the anti-aircraft fire he was attracting. The gunners must have just gotten a fresh supply

Capt Ed Rider at Phan Rang just after completing his 400th B-57 combat mission in the midst of a remarkable career. Rider, who started as an enlisted man, would eventually tally more than 450 combat missions in the Canberra. Then, after a stint as an instructor pilot in the F-111, Rider returned to Southeast Asia to fly A-1 'Sandy' aircraft. He then completed yet another combat tour as a C-130 Command and Control aircraft pilot, where he racked up a further 100 missions (Ed Rider)

of ammo because they were even shooting at his flares. We let down and coordinated altitudes so that we would not run into each other. We made eight vertical dive-bomb passes dropping our "funny bombs" – this was the name that FACs gave to the M35 fire bomb.

'This was the same bomb used to start the firestorms in Tokyo in World War 2. It was a large cluster bomb that opened up a few thousand feet above the ground. The falling bomblets made a fiery waterfall until they hit the ground. Then they spewed out burning white and yellow phosphorus like roman candles. Really something to see at night.

'We stirred up a hornets' nest and the flak was thick – when it got close you could hear it popping like popcorn. We left the "flare ship" to count the burning trucks and then headed for home. Just another routine mission. But we still had our 20 mm ammo left and I hated to take it home. I called the airborne command post and asked if they had any gun targets. They told me to contact a FAC at Tchepone. He had spotted trucks on a ferry crossing the river there.

'We contacted the FAC to coordinate altitudes before we got into his area. We used a secret "base" altitude which changed every 12 hours so that the enemy could not listen in and find out our heights and then set the fuses on his shells for that altitude. That night base altitude was 8000 ft. He said he was at base plus four, or 12,000 ft. I said, "You must mean minus four?" He said no. I asked what the hell he was doing way up there and he replied that his Cessna O-2 wouldn't climb any higher! His flares were floating so high that they did not illuminate the ground, and I had to circle until I got their reflection on the river before I could see it. Bill kept saying something about "bingo" fuel (the minimum required to get back home with 2000 lbs of fuel remaining).

'A few guns were shooting at our sound but not coming close. I knew there were no radar-controlled guns because otherwise we would have been tracked and fired on accurately while we were circling. I finally got it worked out and caught the ferry in the flare reflection on the river and rolled in. I fired about a three-second burst in a 30-degree dive from about 1500 ft. The muzzle flashes lit us up like a Christmas tree and said "Here I am! Shoot me!", and did they ever! Now I knew why that FAC was so high. I pulled about 5Gs to get pointed straight up.

'A small part of my mind registered a red light flashing somewhere in the cockpit but I was too busy to look at it. When I ran out of airspeed at the top and had figured out up from down and was upright again the light was out.

'The FAC was encouraging, saying he had seen lots of hits on the ferry with his night vision scope, so I got set up to go in again. Bill didn't think it was a good idea. Indeed, there were lots of guns protecting the ferry. Most of them were twin barrel 37 mm weapons. I could tell because the "red hot beer cans" streaking past the aeroplane came up in strings of eight. The 37 mm gun fired clips of four rounds, so eight meant twin barrels. I was worried about radar-controlled 57 mm twin barrel units mounted on tracked vehicles that often accompanied large truck convoys, but there was no evidence of them. The most spectacular show was provided by the many 23 mm ZSU units. These were four barrels mounted on a tracked vehicle, and they put out a string of tracers that waved around the sky like a kid playing with a high pressure water hose.

'My normal tactic at night over a well-defended target was to get directly over it at about 8000 ft, roll inverted and pull the nose down to the target, drop my bomb at about 5000 ft and then pull up into a vertical climb (essentially a loop beginning at the top). Just before I ran out of airspeed, I would pull the nose down to level and roll upright. This faked out the gunners because they expected me to be off to the side of the target. I was only vulnerable in the first part of my pull-up. Under very heavy fire I sometimes varied this by not pulling up immediately but by turning 90 degrees and continuing down to low altitude with low power and coasting a few miles away from the target (and the guns). When using my guns, I would dive slightly off to the side, go lower and pull up to a 30-degree dive before firing.

'Bill kept bothering me with this "bingo" fuel business but I didn't have time to discuss it with him. On my second pass, I had to use the same heading as the first run in order to see the target – not a very smart thing to do. When our muzzle flashes lit us up again, I had the feeling that if I pulled up as usual every gun would be aimed at our recovery path, so I didn't pull up. I used my alternate tactic. The sky behind and above us was filled with a spectacular display of fireworks. The FAC was figuratively jumping up and down because we had torched off some of the trucks on the ferry and on the south shore of the river, where the vessel was now resting. Now we did not have to circle around to catch the reflection of the flares to locate the target.

'We still had 600 rounds left – six seconds worth of firing. We could approach from any direction since we could see the burning target. Bill was getting a little shrill now and yelling something about "bingo minus two". I told him I would wind it up with two more passes and then go home. After each pass, when I was pulling 5-6Gs to fake out the gunners, there was that pesky red light in the cockpit. I was so busy trying not to join up with those strings of "red hot beer cans" that I didn't notice what it was. We left the FAC to add up the damage and headed home.

'Relieved of all ordnance and most of its fuel, the B-57 climbed like a homesick angel. In short order we were passing 35,000 ft and I had Bill tighten his oxygen mask and check his system for pressure breathing. As we passed 45,000 ft, we had to forcefully breathe out and just relax and let the pressure blow up our lungs to breathe in. At 53,000 ft we were above over 95 percent of the atmosphere. At that altitude the engines used very little fuel. When we arrived over Pleiku we were 150 nautical miles from home and had just 800 lbs of fuel! Normally, when you land with 2000 lbs that is considered an emergency, but I had been through this many times before, and was only concerned with having enough fuel to taxi to the ramp.

'At that altitude, when you reduce power to idle, it only reduces slightly because the engines cannot reduce fuel consumption very much without flaming out. So, in order to reduce power and expedite our decent, I had to shut off one engine. I shut down the right engine because we would be flying a left hand traffic pattern. Bill was somewhat unhappy. I maintained a 0.84 Mach descent, which meant that the descent got progressively steeper as you got into the denser air at low altitude. This let us down inside the hole of the artillery doughnut at 12,000 ft, keeping us out of the arc of outgoing artillery fire. We were approaching from the north and had to land to the east. Once inside the hole, I extended speed brakes and pushed the nose over to maintain speed. Extending speed brakes at 500 knots is like running into a brick wall, and we were thrown forward hard enough to lock our automatic shoulder harnesses. That is when that pesky red light in the cockpit came on again. This time I determined what it was. It was the low fuel pressure light. This was confirmed by the unwinding of the left engine.

'I was at a critical point in my traffic pattern and had no time to deal with a double engine flameout, so I shut off the left throttle, banked 90 degrees right and pulled the nose around to a heading 180 degrees from the landing heading. Then I rolled inverted, and with about 5Gs pulled the nose down the line of approach lights to the end of the runway and then up the centre of the runway lights, varying the Gs to complete my split-ess at about 1500 ft and at about 400-450 knots.

'While I was busy doing this I asked Bill to inform the tower that we had a double engine flameout and might need a tug to tow us in. Bill had lost his voice and never did make the call. When I levelled off from my split-ess I hit both air-start ignition switches and advanced both throttles to idle. After a 4G break to downwind, I lowered gear and flaps and both engines were making the low moaning sound they made when running at idle. After touchdown I raised the flaps and added power so I could hold the nose up. With 40 knots of headwind it was a long taxi to the far end of the runway. I tried to get Bill interested in betting on whether I could make it all the way into the de-arming area without lowering the nose wheel to the ground. For some reason he was not interested. Anyway, I did make it with the nose wheel in the air, and scared the bejesus out of the de-arming troops.

'While they were de-arming my guns I figured it out. It had to be an inoperative forward boost pump in the main fuel tank. When I went to full power and pulled lots of Gs at Tchepone, one fuel pump could not handle the load and the pressure dropped – not enough, thank God, to flame out the engines. When I extended the speed brakes in my descent to Phan Rang, what little fuel we had left splashed against the forward wall of the tank, uncovering the rear fuel pump and resulting in a flameout. There is an old saying, "There are old pilots and there are bold pilots, but there are no old bold pilots". Not so, but we bold pilots need more luck than most.

'We had enough fuel to make it back to the ramp. After we had parked and deplaned, I made an inspection tour with the crew chief, armed with powerful electric torches. Not a scratch on her! Again, skill and cunning triumphs over ignorance and stupidity. The crew chief brought out the four beers from the tail compartment, ice cold from their sojourn at 50,000 ft, and I spread my maps on the ramp, giving a blow-by-blow description of the mission for my crew chief and armourer. I had an additional audience of most of the crew chiefs and armourers on the ramp who were not otherwise busy. Bill did not want his beer so I drank it too. Needless to say, Bill never got into an aeroplane with me again.'

LOSSES MOUNT

Back home in 1967, the spring turned into what became known as 'The Summer of Love', but for the crews of the 8th and 13th BSs, it could not

A pair of B-57Bs outbound from Phan Rang on a daytime mission, both armed with 750-lb napalm bombs under the wings. 52-1867 has an unusual, non-standard camouflage paint scheme on the drop tanks. When the B-57B/C fleet received Southeast Asian camouflage in 1965-66, the wing tanks were usually left in their standard semi-gloss black paint (*via John DeCillo*)

B-57B 52-1582 of the 8th BS outbound from Phan Rang with a load of napalm bombs under the wings. Unusually, this early production Canberra has the large red beacon on the aft upper fuselage which normally appeared only on the E- and G-models of the B-57. In 1969 this aircraft was converted into a B-57G (*USAF*)

have been a more ironic name for a time of dreadful losses for both squadrons. Valuable crews and irreplaceable aircraft were being lost at an alarming rate.

One of the Canberra's advantages over other tactical aircraft was also one of its greatest disadvantages. Because it could carry so much weaponry, the B-57 was able to make many more passes than the average fighter-bomber. And, as any rookie 'air-to-mud' pilot knows, the more bombing or strafing passes you make, the more chances the bad guys have to hit you.

On 22 April 1967, pilot Maj James Edward Oxley of the 'Grim Reapers' was killed when B-57B 53-3859 took a small arms round in the port wing, causing it to crash near the target some 15 miles southwest of Tan Son Nhut. Oxley's navigator, Capt W E Estabrooks, managed to eject and was rescued. On 3 June, the DOOM Pussy claimed yet another crew, this time from the 8th BS, during an armed reconnaissance mission over one of the southern provinces of North Vietnam. The circumstances of the deaths of pilot Maj Theodore Springston and his navigator Capt Joseph Thomas Kearns, flying B-57B 53-3862, were never determined. They simply failed to return from the mission.

Only five days later, another crew from the 'Yellowbirds' was lost when B-57B 53-3908 was shot down by small arms fire during a night armed reconnaissance mission just ten miles from Phan Rang, near the 4761 ft Hao Chu Hi mountain. Neither crewman, pilot Capt Elwin Harry Busch and navigator 1Lt Peter Whitcomb Morrison, was able to eject in time.

On 19 August B-57B 52-1550 of the 13th BS was shot down with the loss of pilot Maj Richard Michael Secanti and navigator Maj Martin Weigner Andersen while on a CAS mission 25 miles north of Saigon. The aircraft was seen orbiting near its target, believed to be a VC storage area five miles west of Lai Khe, when it was hit by ground fire and crashed. This jet was yet another of the early models brought over from the states, this time from the 3510th Combat Crew Training Wing at Randolph AFB, Texas. Aircraft and crews were becoming increasingly

scarce, and it was plainly obvious to Canberra crews in-theatre that this accelerated rate of attrition could not be sustained indefinitely.

Yet another early-block B-57 (52-1510) was lost with its crew – one killed and one taken prisoner – during a DOOM Pussy mission on 10September. Pilot Maj Norris Overly and his navigator Capt Gaylord Dean Petersen were on a night armed reconnaissance mission in southern North Vietnam when Overly dived to attack an oil tanker on a road northwest of Dong Hoi. The jet was immediately hit in the right engine by AAA and both men ejected, but only Overly survived to be captured.

What followed was both heroic and, for many surviving PoWs, extremely vexing. Overly famously helped nurse critically injured fellow prisoners John McCain and 'Bud' Day back to health in the hated 'Plantation' prison. However, when a group of peace activists came through Hanoi in February 1968, Overly and two other PoWs were released to them, providing a propaganda bonanza to the communists. Although he is criticised to this day by his fellow PoWs, and McCain has refused to speak to him for over 40 years, Overly was able to provide valuable information on the number and treatment of PoWs in the hands of the North when little intelligence on them was known by the US. Three more PoWs were turned over to peace activists on 18 July 1968. The prisoners were under orders from their senior captives that the men were to accept release only in the order of their capture, although some released early were terribly maimed and needed modern medical care.

Following the loss of 52-1510, the 'Redbirds' and 'Yellowbirds' got a six-month respite, with no losses of aircraft or crews from September 1967 through to March 1968. It was not to last, however.

Capt Richard W Hopper and navigator Maj Donald L McHugo of the 8th BS were flying 52-1592 on an armed reconnaissance mission in the *Steel Tiger* area of southern Laos on 25 March when, 20 miles southwest of the A Shau Valley, the jet was hit by AAA in the port engine. Hopper managed to fly the crippled aeroplane back to Da Nang, where he lost control during a treacherous single-engine landing and crashed, killing both crewmen. The B-57B had notoriously bad single-engine performance, and was especially dangerous at low speed and altitude, where it would roll into the dead engine if not handled very carefully.

On 3 April the crew of 52-1586 were luckier when their aircraft – yet another of the elderly replacement machines acquired from the ANG –

was hit by 37 mm flak as it pulled off its second pass over a crossing in the river at Ban Te Bang in southern Laos, again southwest of the A Shau Valley. Although the left wing was severely holed by the flak, pilot Maj Richard Zock managed to get the bomber back to Phan Rang, where he made an emergency landing. A1C T L Tillotson was riding in the back seat as an observer, and he also escaped injury. The aircraft did not fare as well and had to be written off.

While personal art was not as common in the B-57 squadrons as, say, among the F-105 units, many aeroplanes did carry their crews' own markings. For example, *HELL's ANGEL* was the name given to Phan Rang based B-57B 53-3877 in 1967-68. This aircraft was also later converted into a B-57G and it too survived the war (*John DeCillo*)

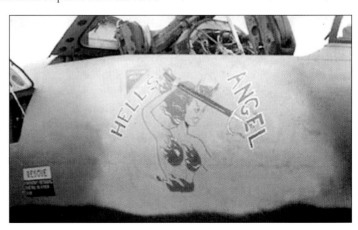

'CENTURION CLUB'

'Our mission', said Bill Maxson, 'was to destroy trucks, plain and simple. The objective was clear – stem the flow of supplies and ammo to the VC and any other NVA forces in South Vietnam'.

From the beginning of the war to the end, near daily, reconnaissance aircraft from every branch of the US armed services returned to their commands with photos of tons and tons of supplies being offloaded from such ports as the huge one at Haiphong and lesser ones like Vinh. These supplies made their way onto Czech trucks and headed down the Trail to the VC in South Vietnam.

No sooner had this B-57B been given a fresh coat of camouflage paint than it got holed by flak! The larger hole is surrounded by soot from an exploding small-calibre round, which entered and severed a high-pressure line, costing pilot J T Stanley his hydraulic pressure. This photo was taken at Phan Rang in 1968 (*Ed Rider*)

'Presumably, air power could make a difference, and we gave it our best effort', said Maxson. 'Even so, as described earlier, the type of weapons we used sure made a difference in how successful we were. For those of us who got there when we still had those "funny bombs", we had a chance to destroy 100 or more trucks and become members of the exclusive "Centurion Club". I was one so fortunate, and took a lot of pride in this accomplishment'.

But Maxson and others saw a downside to having such an exclusive club, whose 'membership dues' were potentially paid for with one's life. Crews were prone to becoming more aggressive than was necessary, and maybe, in Maxson's words, 'pressing the target, getting too low in their dive-bomb runs, making too many passes at heavily defended targets and not having more effective weapons. These were some of the reasons we started losing aircraft and crews.

'I remember well Lt Col Don Klein, a very hot pilot, desperately wanting to get his 100 trucks. In trying they were shot up so bad he and his navigator bailed out "feet wet" and were picked up by one of our Navy destroyers in the South China Sea. Don had extended his tour voluntarily just so he could get into the club! However, he had to go home disappointed, falling only a few trucks short of 100.'

Klein and his navigator, 1Lt R P Erickson, were shot down by 37 mm flak guns on 21 September 1968 while on their fifth run at a truck park near Ban Loumpoum, in southern Laos. They were in B-57B 52-1498, which was the sixth B-model off the production line. This aircraft was yet another of the aged Canberras that were being found at bases across the US and sent to South Vietnam. Used as a development aircraft by Martin and the USAF at Edwards AFB, California, it was converted to combat configuration before being sent into action.

The final loss of 1968 came on 13 December when B-57E 55-4284, flown by Maj T W Dugan and navigator Maj F J McGouldrick, collided with C-123K 'flare ship' 54-0600 of the 56th Special Operations Wing over Ban Nampakhon, in southern Laos. The latter machine was acting as both 'flare ship' and FAC, and having spotted a target at 0330 hrs its crew called in two orbiting B-57s. All three aircraft were operating with

Lt Col Bill Maxson, left, with his navigator, Capt Bob Fuller, of the 8th BS following Maxson's 281st combat mission. This photograph was taken at Phan Rang in February, 1969. Maxson went on to achieve the rank of major general prior to his retirement from the USAF (*Bill Maxson*)

their external lights out, and one of the B-57s struck the C-123 on its attack run. Only the pilot of the Provider survived the collision.

By early 1969, the USAF was struggling to find sufficient B-57Bs to keep its solitary squadron in South Vietnam equipped with an adequate number of serviceable aircraft. Dwindling stocks of Canberras had seen the 13th BS deactivated on 15 January 1968, the unit marking the occasion by flying its 1000th combat sortie. This left the 8th BS as the USAF's sole tactical bomber squadron, sharing the base with eight Royal Australian Air Force Canberra B 20s. Shortly afterwards, the unit cut its ties with the 405th TFW at Clark AFB, becoming an integral part of the 35th TFW on a permanent basis.

Most B-57 missions over the Trail were now being flown by night, although occasional daylight raids were still being made too. And it was one of these, on 22 February 1969, that resulted in the 8th BS suffering its final aircrew combat fatalities in Vietnam. Lt Col Donald Elmer Paxton and his navigator, Maj Charles Macko, were attacking trucks on a road southeast of Ban Kate when their aircraft (52-1532) was hit hard by AAA. Neither crewman had had a chance to eject before the bomber crashed into a hill slope near the road. On 15 March 52-1567 was also hit by ground fire during an attack on a NVA rocket launching position near the A Shau Valley. Lt Col E Tiddy and navigator Maj Michael A De Sousa nursed the jet back to Phan Rang, but then had to crash-land near the airfield when both engines flamed out. This machine had formerly served with both the Nevada and Kentucky ANGs following frontline service with the 38th TBG at Laon AB, in France, during the 1950s.

Just 12 days later, the 8th BS suffered its final loss in Vietnam when 52-1508, crewed by pilot Lt Col Richard W Burkholder and navigator Lt Col H V Wright, was hit by 57 mm flak during a dawn strike on a river ford near Tavouac, in southern Laos. The aircraft was pulling up following its second pass when it was struck, causing a fire to break out in the fuselage. Burkholder managed to nurse the jet to Phu Cat, where he and Wright successfully ejected. This aircraft was the 54th, and last, B-57B to be lost in Southeast Asia since August 1964. Two B-57Es and a B-57C had also been destroyed in combat.

From June 1969 just 13 B-57Bs remained at Phan Rang, as 16 had been sent home over previous months for conversion into B-57Gs. In late September the surviving Canberras and their crews started leaving Phan Rang for Clark, where they would prepare the jets for the long flight back to the US. 52-1551 was the very last B-57B to leave South Vietnam on 15 October, its departure having been delayed because the aircraft required a last minute wing change. Once back home, the weary machines were either turned over to the ANG once again or consigned to the boneyard. According to Robert Mikesh, of the 94 B-57s assigned to the 8th and 13th BSs in 1964-69, 51 were combat losses (including 15 destroyed on the ground). Of the original 47 deployed from Japan, only one (53-3879) remained to the end.

The 8th BS would subsequently return to South Vietnam equipped with the A-37B light attack aircraft as the 8th Attack Squadron. However, the 'Grim Reapers' of the 13th BS would see action once again with their beloved Canberras, although in a variation that the 'old hands' would scarcely recognise.

RAAF CANBERRAS JOIN THE FIGHT

hile Australian troops had been acting as advisors in South Vietnam since 1962, supported by helicopters, Army liaison aircraft and Caribou transports from 1964, the Royal Australian Air Force (RAAF) did not commit tactical jets to the conflict until April 1967. It was then that eight Australian-built Canberra B 20s of No 2 Sqn arrived at Phan Rang to operate under the command of the USAF's 35th TFW. The unit immediately set about making up for lost time, flying sortie after sortie in support of Australian troops, as well as ARVN and American forces.

After discussions with the Seventh Air Force and the 35th BW, it was agreed that the RAAF Canberras would fly up to 16 sorties per day (and in practice sometimes more) against primary and secondary targets with their eight jets. Since the unit arrived in Vietnam during the monsoon season, good flying days were rare. So in the beginning they were often restricted to flying radar-directed *Combat Sky Spot* sorties at night from 20,000 ft. Despite the USAF crews' disdain for these missions, by all accounts the RAAF obtained good results. Part of the reason is that by this stage of the war the technique had been given time for fine-tuning, using better hardware for locating and hitting targets.

During a typical *Combat Sky Spot* mission, the Canberra would take off and transit under radar control to the target area, where the air traffic control would hand the crew off to the *Combat Sky Spot* radar controllers. Either the pilot or navigator would give the controllers details of their

No 2 Sqn Canberra B 20 A84-228 outbound on a mission from Phan Rang. Notable are the field modified bomb racks which replaced the wingtip tanks. Lacking underwing pylons, and finding the external tanks unnecessary, the Aussies modified the wingtips to carry a pair of 500- or 750-lb bombs, thus increasing the bomb load by as much as 25 percent. This particular aircraft was downed by an SA-2 SAM on 14 March 1971 (*via John DeCillo*)

bomb load and bomb ballistics, and they would use these to compute the release point. The *Combat Sky Spot* radar would then guide the Canberra to a point in the sky, the controller giving the crew a five-second countdown to bomb release. The navigator would count the bombs as they fell away from the aircraft and then look for their impact on the ground to make sure that no ordnance had hung up. The Canberra then returned to base. After three months of constant night bombing crews became very proficient at instrument flying.

An RAAF airman examines his bomb load during his pre-flight inspection prior to flying a night mission from Phan Rang. The aircraft's bomb-bay had the conventional two-door arrangement, unlike the B-57's rotary bomb-bay door. Also, the bomb fins are field modifications attached to standard US 500-lb GP bombs (*via John DeCillo*)

A load of six US 500-lb 'box fin' bombs have been modified in the field to accept the 'ring' type fin arrangement used by the RAAF, thus allowing them to fit into the bomb-bay of a Canberra B 20. Also notable are the fuse spinners, which clearly have been cut from sheet metal by armourers in the field. The arrangement obviously worked, because the RAAF crews were renowned for their bombing accuracy (*John DeCillo*)

However, the effectiveness of these missions was proving difficult to determine, and the RAAF aircrews, led by squadron CO Wg Cdr Rolf Aronsen, pressed their USAF superiors to be allowed to switch to low-level daylight operations. Although the 35th TFW 'staffers' were initially sceptical that No 2 Sqn was up to the job, the results the unit achieved in its first few sorties saw crews quickly cleared to fly four of its missions by day. Eventually, the great majority of the squadron's sorties would be flown during daylight.

The Australian Canberras, which flew under the call sign 'Magpie', were virtually identical to the English Electric Canberra B 2 – the same design that sired all the B-57 models, although the B 20 did not have the underwing hardpoints and pylons of the USAF Canberras. However, because the distances to their targets were relatively short, alleviating the need for tip tanks, field-modified bomb racks were quickly manufactured to replace the tanks. This gave the Canberra B 20 a bomb load of up to eight 1000-lb bombs, or just about any combination up to that weight.

The standard bomb-bay layout saw six bombs hung from two triple racks, but due to repeated instances of hung ordnance, the RAAF devised an alternate system that put six bombs on individual racks within the bay. The B 20 had a conventional bomb-bay with two quick-opening doors, unlike the unique rotary door system used by the B-57.

Another difference was that the RAAF Canberra crews excelled at low-altitude level bombing, whereas their USAF brethren relied on dive-bombing tactics and strafing. The Canberra B 20 also lacked guns. However, they could swoop in low, deliver their ordnance on target and be out of range before enemy gunners could draw a bead on them. It was obviously a good tactic because in four years of war No 2 Sqn lost just two aircraft.

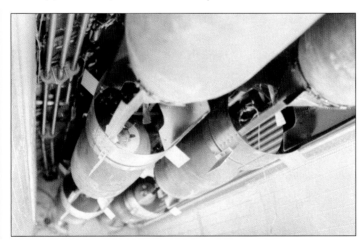

A Canberra B 20 crew successfully deliver their ordnance during a canal-busting mission in the Mekong Delta in 1968 (*RAAF*)

With the USAF and RAAF Canberra squadrons sharing a base at Phan Rang as well as a wing command, they often shared technicians, maintenance people and armourers as well. The rationale behind this was that they were fighting the same war, so they did whatever was required to get the sorties flown and the bombs on target.

To aid in their level bombing, the Australian Canberras were fitted with the Green Satin Doppler navigation system – a bombsight in which the navigator lay prone in the Perspex nose of the jet and a bomb intervalometer that released each weapon with very accurate spacing.

Like their US counterparts, the Canberra's range gave the jet a great advantage over faster strike aircraft. If the primary target was not available, the crew could follow a FAC to another location, be handed off to another FAC for a new target or loiter in one area for targets of opportunity, sometimes requiring only one bomb per target. According to an account by No 2 Sqn vet Rod Farquhar, 'During bad weather and especially in the monsoon season when dive-bombing by USAF aeroplanes was not an option, we could go in under the clouds, in extreme cases as low as 800 ft'.

The squadron flew its first sorties on 23 April with all eight aircraft, the Canberras dropping 42 500-lb bombs on 11 targets spread almost two-thirds the length of South Vietnam from II Corps in the north to deep into IV Corps in the Mekong Delta. The latter area was where No 2 Sqn would expend more than two-thirds of its ordnance during the years it was deployed to Vietnam.

Another thing the Australian unit shared with the USAF Canberra squadrons was old bombs. The 'Redbirds' and 'Yellowbirds' never ran out of ordnance even when there were supposed 'bomb shortages' in-country. That was because the B-57s, like the A-1 Skyraiders, could carry old World War 2-era box-fin bombs just as well as newer weapons, and in some cases they were a better fit. In the beginning, No 2 Sqn employed bombs that had been dredged up from dumps all over Australia. Most of these were of the British 'round fin' design and had been in storage since

A pilot and navigator pose with the last World War 2 era 500-lb 'round fin' bomb to be dropped by No 2 Sqn in Vietnam (*RAAF*)

the end of World War 2, although they were still just as potent as ever. RAAF statistics show that 27,568 of the old bombs were used in total, and after these were gone standard USAF weapons were expended, most of these being 750-lb M117 bombs. In order to accommodate the longer American ordnance modifications to the bomb-bay had to be made, after which a standard load typically consisted of four 750–lb bombs internally and a 750 'pounder' on each wingtip.

USAF FAC Col Larry Van Pelt worked targets in southern Laos, and he had a special admiration for

the RAAF crews. He specifically asked for them to destroy a road bridge he and his observer discovered hidden away on a branch of the Trail;

'The Ho Chi Minh Trail in Southeast Asia was really a whole network of trails – from truck-worthy roads to bicycle paths and, finally, to narrow footpaths. The enemy used this network to bring all sorts of supplies and weapons all the way from Hanoi and Haiphong down into the southernmost parts of South Vietnam. Part of that network fed right into the area that I patrolled as a FAC flying OV-10 Bronco aircraft.

'There was a part of that trail that really puzzled both me and the rest of the FACs. We could see a well used, narrow trail adjacent to a steep, heavily forested canyon which resumed again on the other side of the canyon in mountainous terrain. The canyon was steep and deep, so there had to be a bridge spanning it that connected the two trails. But thick jungle trees covered it, and the approach to it, keeping the bridge from our view.

'Lt Steve Williams and I took it as a personal challenge – we were determined to find the exact location of that bridge so we could destroy it. The bridge was located in enemy territory well beyond the Army's artillery range, so we couldn't use their big guns to go after it, or even blast away the trees so we could locate the crossing more precisely. We searched for the bridge on several occasions, orbiting at a safe altitude away from small arms fire and scanning the area with high-powered binoculars. Steve and I gradually narrowed our search, and one day, with Steve in my back seat, we concurred that we had found the precise location. Noting the map coordinates, we passed this information onto the other FACs so when they were flying they could confirm our discovery. None of them could confirm it, however. With a bit of tongue in cheek, it became known as "The Invisible Van-Williams Bridge".

'Steve and I weathered the cynicism and turned our energies toward convincing higher headquarters that we had found a critical weakness in a part of the Ho Chi Minh Trail, and that it should be bombed. After much pleading, we finally convinced headquarters to spare a couple of

No 2 Sqn pilots and navigators walk along the Phan Rang flightline after flying in from RAAF Base Butterworth, in Malaysia, during a largescale jet swap (*via Andrew Thomas*)

A No 2 Sqn Canberra B 20 bombs a VC trail near Phu Cat in the southern Mekong Delta in November 1969. The aircraft was being flown by squadron CO, Wg Cdr Jack Boast, and navigator Sqn Ldr Frank Lonie at the time (*via Andrew Thomas*)

Armourers and an anonymous Canberra pilot share a joke after the 10,000th bomb (in this case an elderly 500-lb weapon) uploaded by No 2 Sqn in Vietnam had been attached to the wing pylon of this B 20 (*via Andrew Thomas*)

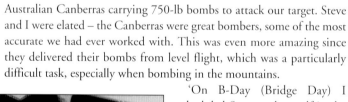

Australian Canberras carrying 750-lb bombs to attack our target. Steve and I were elated – the Canberras were great bombers, some of the most accurate we had ever worked with. This was even more amazing since they delivered their bombs from level flight, which was a particularly difficult task, especially when bombing in the mountains.

'On B-Day (Bridge Day) I scheduled Steve and myself in the same aeroplane so we could direct the attack. With our binoculars (and a nice camera provided by the intelligence folks) in hand, we got airborne in our trusty, two-seat Bronco in plenty of time to be over the target area well before the Canberras arrived. After relocating the bridge (only a few feet of it was visible through a hole in the tree canopy) we took a few pictures – we wanted some photos of both before and after to convince the naysayers. When the Canberras arrived I

Canberra B 20 A84-231 drops its ordnance on a VC 'cement factory' in the Mekong Delta. This aircraft was lost on 3 November 1970 during a *Combat Sky Spot* strike, the wreckage of the jet remaining undiscovered in the Vietnamese jungle until April 2009 (*via Andrew Thomas*)

directed them to orbit overhead while I described the target area and made sure they could see both it and us. They were a little bit suspicious, maybe even miffed, as they had been sent to destroy a bridge and all they could see were heavily forested mountains.

'When they were ready to make their bomb run I told them I would identify the exact desired impact point by marking the target with a smoke rocket. With a well aimed rocket, a small white smoke cloud erupted right where I wanted them to bomb. I then uttered the words of a good FAC – "Hit my smoke". I had directed them to drop their bombs one at a time. This gave us an opportunity to clear the tree cover, exposing the bridge for final destruction. The tactic worked perfectly, as the 750-lb bombs were good at clearing trees. After a couple of passes the elusive Van-Williams Bridge was clearly exposed. It was easily 100 ft long and about three or four feet wide, built out of wood.

'The Canberra crews were now excited too. Up until then they thought they were just bombing trees. Now they could see a *real* bridge across the *real* Ho Chi Minh Trail. There was no need to put more smoke rockets on the target – the navigators could now see the target clearly. I circled the bridge so Steve could get some pictorial evidence and then I cleared the bombers in for the knockout blows. With just a few passes the Van-Williams Bridge collapsed a couple of hundred feet down into a pile of sticks at the bottom of the ravine. I thought, "Well done, my Aussie friends".

'The VC were not too happy about our achievement, as the many muzzle flashes from the area confirmed. Now they would have to carry their large supply loads on their backs down, down, down into the canyon and then up, up, up, instead of just walking across a bridge – at least until they built another one.'

FIRST LOSS

It would be more than three years before the RAAF lost its first Canberra crew in Southeast Asia. On 3 November 1970, A84-231, flying as 'Magpie 91', was on a night *Combat Sky Spot* mission and had just delivered its 500-lb bombs from 22,000 ft on a target in Quang Nam Province, southwest of Da Nang and just east of the Laotian border. The target was believed to be a concentration of North Vietnamese

Flg Off Michael Herbert was at the controls of A84-231 when it went missing on 3 November 1970 (*RAAF*)

Plt Off Robert Carver was A84-231's navigator during the ill-fated 3 November 1970 *Combat Sky Spot* mission (*RAAF*)

No 2 Sqn personnel come together for a group photograph at Phan Rang on the eve of leaving Vietnam for good on 4 June 1971 (*via Andrew Thomas*)

regulars, or a possible NVA headquarters, the enemy having crossed over from the Laotian border 15 miles away.

After dropping its bombs at 2022 hrs local time in poor weather conditions, the aircraft had turned about 80 degrees to the right off its target run-in heading, commencing its return to Phan Rang, when it disappeared from radar. The location of the crew, pilot Flg Off Michael Herbert and navigator Plt Off Robert Carver, and the wreckage of 'Magpie 91' were unknown for 39 years. Finally, in April 2009 an Australian Army History Unit, supported by Vietnamese forensic specialists, discovered the Canberra B 20 southeast of the original target. Three months later the crew's remains were also discovered, and both men were returned to Australia for burial on 31 August 2009.

It is still unknown what caused 'Magpie 91' to crash, with speculation ranging from NVA AAA or a surface-to-air missile (SAM) to a hung bomb or friendly long-range artillery fire arcing through A84-231's flight path in the target area.

The second, and last, loss of an RAAF Canberra B 20 occurred less than six months later, and its demise illustrates just how much the battlefield had changed since the first American B-57s had arrived almost seven years earlier. On 14 March 1971, Wg Cdr John Downing, CO of No 2 Sqn, and his navigator, Flt Lt A Pinches, were downed in A84-228 at 0245 hrs when the bomber was struck by an SA-2 SAM (one of two that were fired at the aircraft) not far from the abandoned US Marine Corps base at Khe Sanh. By now the NVA were crossing the DMZ almost at will, and had moved heavy anti-aircraft defences well into South Vietnamese territory.

Both men ejected, Wg Cdr Downing (who was flying his 100th combat mission) recalling, 'My first sensation after pulling the blind was that of tumbling and still clutching the blind. I released my grip and

This specially decorated M117 750-lb weapon was the 76,389th, and last, bomb dropped by No 2 Sqn in anger in Vietnam. A84-244, crewed by pilot Flg Off D Smith (left) and navigator Flg Off P Murphy (right), performed this historic mission on 30 May 1971 (*via Andrew Thomas*)

The remains of the last two Australian servicemen missing in action from the war in Vietnam were returned to their homeland on 31 August 2009. Four months earlier, the wreckage of A84-231 had been found in remote jungle near the border with Laos after a search conducted by an Australian Army History Unit. Three months later the remains of the airmen were found, and then identified by Australian and Vietnamese forensic specialists. Official interest in finding and repatriating Australia's missing war dead was revived in 2007 after a veterans' organisation found the bodies of two soldiers. Another soldier was found that year, with a fourth found in 2008. The remains of Flg Off Michael Herbert and Plt Off Robert Carver, both aged 24 when they perished, were returned to RAAF Base Richmond in a C-130H, RAAF airmen from the Federation Guard forming an honour guard while the bearer party from No 2 Sqn carried the remains of their comrades to waiting biers (*RAAF*)

skydived to stabilise. I looked behind me, saw the ejection seat tumbling, and then felt the back of the parachute opening'. Both men landed safely, although Downing broke one of his kneecaps when he hit a rocky ridge and Pinches had had four of the vertebrae in his spine crushed when he ejected. They had to spend a harrowing night on the ground separated from one another, and in danger of being caught by the VC or NVA at any time. Finally, some 27 hours after the aircraft had been shot down both men were safely picked up and soon hospitalised.

Within weeks of this loss, the RAAF Canberra contingent was ordered to pull out of Phan Rang and return to Australia – the last USAF B-57Bs had left the theatre in October 1969. On 4 June 1971, five days after flying the last of almost 12,000 sorties, No 2 Sqn left for home. During its time in South Vietnam the unit had been credited with the destruction of 7000 buildings, 10,000 bunkers, 1000 sampans and 36 bridges, and it had killed an unknown number of NVA and VC personnel.

ENTER THE DRAGON

The B-57G, developed under the *Tropic Moon III* programme, was arguably the deadliest tactical jet yet to be deployed in Southeast Asia. Everything about it was secret, and that, coupled with the fact that it only operated at night, meant that the B-57G was a very low-profile aircraft in the later years of the war. It carried state-of-the-art electronics gear and was the first aircraft to use the new laser-guided bomb (LGB) as a standard part of its weapons load. In addition, the crews now had a way to see in the dark with low light level television (LLLT) and infrared radar (IR) pictures in real time. It was no longer possible to quickly pull some branches over a truck to hide it at night, since the IR could see the hot engine right through the foliage.

Throughout its career the B-57 was routinely used as a nocturnal intruder, yet the aeroplane when configured as a bomber had no radar, let alone any other avionics that would help a crew locate and attack targets at night. Without the 'flare ships', the Canberras were all but blind. With the introduction of the B-57G near the end of the aircraft's useful life with the USAF, it finally became a genuine night intruder.

In June 1969, 16 B-57Bs were sent to the Martin plant in Baltimore where they were to undergo a major refit under a dual contract with Westinghouse. A bulbous radome and an ungainly chin fairing were added to the Canberra. These housed forward-looking radar as well as the business ends of the IR and LLLT cameras and an early laser rangefinder that was used in this case for targeting newly developed LGBs. Aesthetically, the B-57G was not about to win any prizes, but somehow the ugly look went with the sinister nature of its business. After deployment to the combat zone, crews flying the aircraft wore a patch showing a three-headed dragon with white, red and green eyes, each of which signified a separate weapons system.

USAF acceptance flights for the B-57G were carried out from the Martin Baltimore plant in October 1969, after which crews were posted to the 4424th Combat Crew Training Squadron (CCTS)/15th TFW at MacDill AFB, Florida, to commence their transition onto the new Canberra variant. The B-57Gs were subsequently assigned to the 13th BS 'Grim Reapers', which had been reactivated in February 1970. In September of that year the unit returned to Southeast Asia, where it was based at Ubon RTAB under the command of Lt Col Paul R Pitt as part of the predominantly F-4 Phantom II-equipped 8th TFW. The unit's new mounts no longer boasted guns in the wings, but they did continue to carry the old, but still effective, incendiary cluster 'funny bombs' internally, as well as four 260-lb fragmentation bombs or 500-lb Paveway I LGBs under the wings.

The three-headed dragon insignia worn by B-57G crews. Each of the three heads has different colour eyes, each symbolising a different weapons system on the aircraft. Almost hidden in the curl of the dragon's tail is the Westinghouse logo, the firm having developed the advanced new systems fitted in the jet. And company 'tech reps' performed much of the avionics maintenance on the G-models in the field

Top Right
B-57G 53-3929 climbs out on a training mission from MacDill AFB near Orlando, Florida. During the 13th BS's rigorous accelerated transition to the new G-model, it came under the control of the 1st TFW. Most of these missions were flown unarmed or with conventional practice weapons. After the aircraft were deployed to the combat zone, LGBs were carried under the wings almost exclusively (*USAF*)

Weapons Systems Operator (WSO) Capt R K Markel, was one of the first crewmen to take the new jet into combat. He did not think that the B-57G was the 'super machine' that Martin touted it to be, although he confirmed that some of its gadgets were helpful;

'To carry the various sensors, the B-57G was considerably modified from its original aerodynamic configuration. It was given more powerful engines, but even with these, increased drag from the huge radome considerably reduced its flight performance. Compared to its unmodified predecessors, it was a dog. The reconnaissance altitude of 5000 ft that we were forced to fly at because of the aircraft's sensors was considerably lower than optimum for fuel consumption. It had no in-flight refuelling capability, so mission time (and, consequently, time on target) was severely limited. Our missions normally lasted two to three hours, with about an hour in the target area.

'The sensor range was limited. Often, by the time a target was spotted, we were past bomb release point, and I could not find the target when we returned. The Moving Target Indicator (MTI) was a dead loss – this was an ongoing problem with the aeroplane that was never solved. The ECM gear was nice, but unnecessary. If there were any radar-directed weapons in the parts of Laos that we patrolled, none of them ever lined up on any of the aircraft in which I flew. I was told sensor maintenance was difficult, but other than the MTI, in 140 missions I never had a sensor fail. Indeed,

The crew of the first B-57G to arrive in Southeast Asia is greeted at Ubon RTAB, Thailand, in September 1970. Their aircraft was soon joined by ten more G-models, these jets being assigned to the 13th BS. The unit was in turn controlled by the 8th TFW (*USAF*)

I never arrived at the jet on the ramp to find it was not ready because of an aircraft or equipment problem. Furthermore, I was told that the LGBs had a failure rate of three percent. I bettered that average. Every LGB I dropped guided successfully. Our groundcrews were absolutely fantastic. Whatever shortcomings our equipment had, those people were up to taking care of it.'

Since the B-57G had ushered in so much new technology, 13th BS groundcrews at Ubon were a mix of both USAF personnel and civilian 'tech reps' from various contractors associated with the specialist mission equipment fitted to the jet. Once

in the air, the B-57G was just as much a challenge for aircrew too as they got to grips with learning how to 'laze' a target for destruction with an LGB. The devising of tactics and techniques for the new 'smart' bombs required a good deal of trial and error, as Capt Markel recalled;

'Combining both dropping and guiding the bomb required some doing. The problem we had was that the bomb lagged behind the aircraft and, in level flight, the sensors could not look back far enough to follow it to impact. The sensor could look forward and down about 90 degrees, but could not follow the bomb behind the aircraft. This precluded holding the laser on target to complete the strike.

'To be effectively guided, the bomb's control surfaces required release at a speed greater than 250 knots. The solution was for the sensor operator to acquire the target and notify the pilot, who would then shove the power forward to reach an airspeed above 250 knots. At "bombs away", he would yank back the power and the stick, creating a climb and inevitable stall. When the aircraft pitched nose down, the sensors could look far enough to the rear long enough to guide and follow the bomb drop through to impact, while maintaining laser direction during stall recovery. Not elegant, but it worked!'

This rather bizarre and, when under fire, dangerous manoeuvre was adopted by many B-57G crews. Following combat experience with the aircraft, later designators, such as those used on the F-111, would be mounted on a gimbal that could swivel through almost 180 degrees.

TEAMWORK WITH THE AC-130

Even with all the new avionics that allowed B-57G crews to 'see' in the dark, they continued to work side-by-side with the C-130, only now instead of 'flare ships' they usually operated with AC-130A Spectre gunships. For one thing, the AC-130 could spot targets with its own side-mounted laser designator and then start an orbit that kept the laser beam on the target for as long as was needed for the B-57G to drop its bomb and see it guided to the target.

The AC-130A preceded the B-57G into theatre, the gunships being based at Ubon and boasting the same sensors as the Canberra. A major difference between the two aircraft, however, was that the Spectre had one crewman assigned to each sensor – that is, it had individual operators for the Forward Looking Infrared (FLIR), radar, LLLT and ECM equipment, as well as a dedicated navigator. The Spectre also had a tape recorder onboard to record all the outputs from the various mission equipment, as well as a crewman dedicated to the recorder's operation.

Another difference between the two types centred on the ordnance that the aircraft brought to bear. The Spectres had side-firing 20 mm Gatling guns and 40 mm Bofors cannons, both of which were effective weapons, but they were not as destructive as an accurately dropped 500-lb LGB from an orbiting B-57G. The Spectres also had a 105 mm howitzer on board, but it suffered from a lack of accuracy. This problem would be corrected in later versions of the AC-130, turning the 105 mm gun into a devastating weapon. Commenting on the differences between the Spectre and the B-57G, Capt Markel said;

'The "Specs" had five to seven guys aboard doing what the one guy in the back seat of the B-57G handled by himself. It could be strongly argued that with their additional sets of eyes they should have been able to do a better job of finding targets than a lone WSO in the back seat of a Canberra. They flew higher (9000 ft) and slower than the B-57. Some suggested that the reason the Spectre flew higher was that the USAF was concerned about the AC-130A's vulnerability to AAA at a lower level, where it was less able to take evasive action than we were in the B-57G. When the gunships found a target, they could circle it and keep it in sight rather than overfly and possibly lose it when they returned, as often happened to the "fast-movers", including the B-57s.

'While he may not have been the first to whom the idea occurred that the "Specs" and the "Redbirds" (the 13th BS call sign) could usefully team up, the "Birds" supplying the bombs and the 'Specs' the guidance, Canberra pilot Capt Mike Thorn was the first to do something about it.

'The AC-130s carried an ultraviolet light generator, which emitted a light that was, presumably, invisible to unfriendly eyes on the ground, but which lit up the countryside pretty well for the low light sensors aboard the Spectre. It also showed up well on the low-light scopes of the B-57G. Mike, who was the 13th BS's youngest pilot, figured there might be a way to use it for "Spec"/"Redbird" truck bombing. He and I discussed it. I was interested.'

Markel and Thorn also made two orientation flights with the Spectres to assess their capabilities, the latter recalling;

'I flew with the "Specs" in order to get the pilot's point of view of the missions we were conducting, but I did not enjoy it very much. Being a typical jet pilot, I was not accustomed to the thrumming and throbbing of the AC-130's four propellers and, to make matters worse, I could not see out of the aircraft. So, to avoid being airsick, I joined the young airman hanging out the back of the aircraft to get some fresh air. The airman's job was to watch for ground fire, while mine was simply to avoid the loss of my lunch. I did pretty well at that until I realised that I was hanging out over open space but was not tied to the aircraft in any way!

'The second time I flew with the "Specs" I fared no better in the area of airsickness, but at least I made sure that I was tied to the aircraft. Unfortunately, the metal container on which I was leaning was a flare box – a fact I did not realise until flares shot out of my armpit! I decided that two rides had provided all the information and experience I needed.'

Thorn worked out tactics he thought would work and then went over them with Markel and a Spectre pilot. One night over Laos, due to some under-the-table scheduling, Thorn and Markel found themselves in the same piece of sky as the AC-130. Markel recalled;

'He called us to say that he had a hard target that he wanted some help with, so he gave us coordinates. I slapped them into the Doppler and we headed in. Approaching the target area, we asked "Spec" to "sparkle". Sure enough, a huge bright spot appeared on my LLLT screen. At the same time the "Spec" fired 20 mm tracer rounds at the target, providing a visual reference for the pilot. Mike shoved the power forward, I lined up the cross hairs on the middle of the light spot, set the bomb switches and gave the "Spec" a countdown to bombs away. I never saw the target. It was that simple. Mike and I then went back to normal road watching. The next day, Mike went to the "Spec" debrief. They showed him the tape playback of the destruction of a road grader with our bomb – so far

A completely 'clean' B-57G departs Ubon during the day. The aircraft is not only devoid of weapons, it has had its pylons removed as well. This jet may be on a ferry flight to Clark AB, in the Philippines, for maintenance or other reasons, hence the fact the drag-inducing pylons have been left on the ground (*Joe English*)

B-57G 53-3929 is seen in the maintenance area at Ubon RTAB. The G-model carried state-of-the-art avionics and target acquisition systems that made it something of a maintenance nightmare for crews that worked 12-hour days, often seven days a week, in the tropical heat. They were aided by 'tech reps' from the contractors who had a stake in the success of the aircraft's then-futuristic systems, such as LGBs that rarely missed their targets (*Knowles via Robert Mikesh Archive*)

as we knew, this type of close cooperation with the B-57G was a first for the Spectres.'

Despite its configuration for night operations, declassified records show that B-57Gs flew a number of successful daytime CAS missions that suppressed enemy encirclement of troops on the ground in Cambodia. Although details are sketchy at best, in these missions LGBs were exchanged for Mk 82 500-lb 'Snakeye' retarded bombs that were optimised for low level attacks.

TANK BUSTING ON THE TRAIL

Nick Paldino, a 1965 US Naval Academy Graduate (at that time, one in eight graduates had to go to another branch of the military service), was a B-57G pilot with the 13th BS who enjoyed a long career with the USAF. Indeed, many years after his service in Vietnam he made a valuable contribution to the weapons system development for the then-new Panavia Tornado whilst serving as an exchange officer with the Royal Air Force. Paldino recalled;

'The G-model was really a research and development test bed for smart weapons. The mission debriefers were always from the contractors – Raytheon for the FLIR, etc. They would do all the maintenance on them. It was a tremendous opportunity for them, as they had a real war to test these things in. That was the genesis of all the smart weapons you see today. All that equipment was classified then. There were only 34 officers in the squadron. I went to Eglin and was assigned to LGB systems before we were deployed to Vietnam.

'At that stage in the air war (1971) it was all about the numbers – number of sorties flown, tonnage of bombs dropped, number of trucks destroyed – yet most of that didn't mean anything to the state of the conflict in general. By this time the NVA was bringing tanks down the Trail, and when an AC-130 got one they couldn't take out, they called us in. The AC-130 would have the target marked and the bombing solution all ready for us, and they would even tell us when to release. We were slaved to them. I flew 38 missions and I worked with them on four occasions, but we were never specifically "fragged" as part of the mission orders to work directly with the AC-130.'

The B-57Gs went about their nocturnal business alone most of the time. They would be given an area of operations along the Trail and would eliminate everything that

moved within it. According to Paldino, it was not unusual for the occasional elephant to wind up in the crosshairs, since they showed up as a huge, hot target on the FLIR, not unlike a tank;

'We usually carried four LGBs on the wings and four of incendiary cluster bombs internally. Targets varied, and we were "fragged" very generally. We were given an area to operate in and we went after targets of opportunity. We'd go into the area – usually measuring around 100 square miles – on the Trail and start working. We'd be "fragged"

Capt Nick Paldino (left) and his WSO, Capt Ron Silvia, who is sporting a leather Eastern Bloc flying helmet, are kitted out for their final departure from Thailand on 12 April 1972 (*via Nick Paldino*)

based on intel from sensors and other sources. You never knew what you might encounter. Sometimes you'd fly for two-and-a-half hours and not see anything, but other times there was all kinds of traffic.

'You were often depending on your backseater to determine whether you hit something or not. We loitered at 200 mph. In those days, picking out a target on that old-fashioned FLIR, we didn't have the image definition to tell an elephant in the woods from a tank. We wouldn't know until we flew directly over it. Then I would hit the Inertial Navigation System button, fly out for four or five minutes, then turn back to that heading, and if it was an elephant it wouldn't have sped up very much. However, if it was a tank or truck it would usually have moved quite a distance in that time. I would then pitch up using the computer ballistics to tell me when to release. It was like toss bombing, releasing on the pitch-up, and the end results were usually accurate. By the time the WSO started lasing and the bomb started looking, the weapon would still have sufficient time to correct its trajectory.

'On this particular mission, we went through all that and then the tank started to speed up. The bomb had only 30 seconds from release before it hit as we were only at 3000 ft. You could see the LGB correcting itself as the tank sped up, attempting to run from the bomb. The weapon hit

CHERRY BOMBER! was the name given to B-57G 52-1580, which is shown here with its full load of M35/36 'funny bombs'. The yellow stripe indicates an explosive, while the red stripe is the mark for an incendiary bomb – the M35/36 was both (*James Pickles*)

about six feet behind the tank, and I saw it flip "ass-over-teakettle" about three times. Howver, when we got back to base they only gave us a probable for it! The intel people said that since the tank hadn't blown up it wasn't destroyed. The same folks told us that if we came back with any bombs still on the jet they wouldn't give us credit for completing a combat sortie.'

The G-models may have been ugly, but their capabilities and their accuracy were spectacular. That, coupled with the highly classified

nature of their 'magical' systems, cultivated a sinister mystique about them. And to some aircrews flying the aircraft it seemed as if everybody wanted to catch a glimpse of the 'dragon' at work. For the B-57G crews, though, the nights turned into seemingly endless duels with flak batteries in the dark, which prevented them from enjoying their own show.

In April 1971, WSO Capt Dick Fontaine participated in a mission with his regular pilot, Capt Mike Thorn, where they encountered a FAC who wanted to see the aeroplane and its famous "funny bombs" in action. Fontaine and Thorn did not disappoint, as the former explained;

'I don't recall the exact take-off time, but it was probably not a late night, more like 2200-2300 hrs. We flew out from Ubon on the 040 radial – my personal favourite – which led to a good radar checkpoint inside the *Steel Tiger East* border within Laos. Just prior to that point, we called "Moonbeam" – the circling C-130 control ship – to ask for clearance into the working area. We descended from 19,000 ft down to 500-1000 ft above high terrain.

'Sometime just prior to reaching our target area between "Delta 53" and "Delta 57", northwest of the DMZ, a FAC out of Nakhon Phanom RTAB asked if we were going to drop "funny" bombs. We carried four of these M36 incendiary cluster bomb units in the bomb-bay and two Mk 82 LGBs on the wing stations. We told him okay, as he wanted to watch because they were pretty spectacular when they went off. The FAC orbited north and above us while we were trolling along an east-west road that ran in and out of the tree canopy, and I got a mover on my LLLT screen. There wasn't much time from acquisition to release, but it was still long enough for a 37 mm flak gun to pop off some rounds'

Thorn takes up the story;

'I saw the flak first, as Dick was largely head down in his scope. I probably mumbled, but in a calm way of course, something along the lines of "Fuck me!" I pulled back on the stick, not on purpose, but in reaction to the fireballs coming at us, and the M36 released early. It was a case of "Oh hell, missed him", as the bomb opened at about 1500 ft and the incendiaries landed in the trees below. There must have been a truck park down there as all sorts of stuff started blowing up, so what the hell. We kept making re-attacks, with that 37 mm gun popping off "baseballs" at us, until we were out of bombs. The flak battery had kept me rather busy as Dick acquired the targets for our ordnance.

'The FAC, who was ecstatic, had a starlight scope that allowed him to confirm all of the Battle Damage Assessment requirements for the mission. He counted ten trucks destroyed and numerous secondary explosions. He also told us that he had enjoyed the show. We exited the area, checked out with "Moonbean" and returned to Ubon pretty pumped, but in a controlled manner, over the results of our

Capt Mike Thorn straps into the cockpit of his B-57G for his last combat sortie of the war. Thorn had flown approximately 100 missions in the B-57 up to this point. Before that, he flew 125 *Arc Light* missions in the B-52. Thorn, then the junior pilot in the 13th BS (an indication of the wealth of experience among the crews), finished his war with just under 1000 hours of combat flying to his name (*via Mike Thorn*)

flight. The next morning the boss (squadron CO Lt Col Paul Pitt) told us we "did good". In fact, we could do no wrong for the next month.

Thorn recalled another night mission from that same month;

'This one stands out *clearly* in my memory. Further south over the "Catcher's Mitt" near "Delta 47" we found a target-rich environment of trucks, and kept re-attacking it on a north-south axis. There were seven 23 mm guns down there, and they figured out our approach on the second pass, lobbing volleys at us each time – that came to 343 rounds per minute. On the fourth or fifth pass, heading south, we were hit in the right wing, and we had a fire warning light. As I pulled the engine back, I asked Dick for our minimum descent altitude (MDA) in order to stay above the terrain. He calmly responded that he would check on that.

'As I was descending, and avoiding the rounds coming up at us (it was like a feeding frenzy for the guys on the ground), I somewhat testily mentioned that I could really use that MDA. Dick responded that he was working on it and, after what seemed like an interminably long time, provided it. We levelled out approximately 300-500 ft below that level and *slooooowly* climbed back up. By then we had fallen low enough that the guys on the ground could not really find us through the karst and tree canopy, and we flew away in a slow climb back to base. My heart rate was probably in range of 150+ beats per minute.'

'I think my hands were shaking, and I had a hard time lighting a cigarette on climb out', explained Dick Fontaine.

Only one B-57G was lost in Southeast Asia, in a tragic midair collision at night with an O-2 Skymaster FAC over southern Laos on 12 December 1970. Flying B-57G 53-3931 was squadron CO Lt Col Paul Pitt and WSO Lt Col Ed Buschette, who was the 13th BS's chief sensor operator. The men believed that they had been hit by anti-aircraft fire, and flying only 25 miles west of the DMZ near the Trail at the time, this was a logical conclusion. Ejecting near Ban Vangthon, the pair spent a terrifying night on the ground within earshot of enemy troops, before being airlifted out the following day from separate hiding places.

In the event, *Nail* FAC O-2A 67-21428 of the 504th Tactical Air Support Group, flown by 1Lt Thomas Allen Duckett with observer Maj Owen George Skinner, failed to return to its base at Nakhon Phanom that night. The following day the mostly intact wreckage of the O-2 was found on the ground. It was reported that emergency radio contact was made with someone in the area, but neither man was ever found. It is possible that their survival radios were taken by the enemy in an attempt to 'sucker' rescue forces into the area. Both men remain listed as missing.

Transferred from Ubon to Clark in April 1972 following a 20-month tour of duty, the surviving B-57Gs were duly transferred to the 190th Tactical Bombardment Group (TBG) of the Kansas ANG upon their return home. After two more years of service with the ANG, the B-57Gs were placed in storage and then disposed of. Not a single example of the G-model escaped the scrapper's torch.

AND IN THE END . . .

When it was all over, 39 crewmen were dead, two were PoWs and 60 Canberras of all types had been lost. In the grand scheme of things, these numbers seem small – that is, until it is considered that these were from only

A groundcrewman refills the liquid oxygen bottles on 53-3889 *MIDNIGHT COWBOY*, which was named by its crew chief, Sgt Pete Knoop. Although it is difficult to see in this photograph, the bomb-bay is loaded with what appear to be M117 750-lb general purpose bombs, rather than the more usual four M35/36 incendiary cluster bombs (*James Pickles*)

B-57G 53-3878 departs Ubon RTAB on 12 April 1972, along with the rest of the 13th BS, thus ending the Canberra's long operational tenure in Southeast Asia. Of the 16 B-57Gs made, 11 were sent into combat but only one was lost. The remaining five were used in the US for training and weapons system testing and development (*via Joe English*)

A ghostly light is cast over a pair of 13th BS B-57Gs, which have been readied for their night missions from Ubon RTAB. The crew van to the right has just delivered its passengers to their aeroplane, which the groundcrews had spent the day attending to, repairing maintenance 'squawks', doing pre-flight duties such as replenishing the oxygen supply and bombing the aircraft up (*via James Pickles*)

two squadrons of American aircraft and a half-squadron of RAAF Canberras. These numbers do not include those killed or maimed on the ground in mortar attacks and the Bien Hoa flightline explosion. When all of this is taken into account, these are grim statistics indeed.

Retired Col Fleming Hobbs, who was there from the beginning as lead navigator on the first B-57 combat mission over North Vietnam, succinctly distilled the contributions of the 'Yellowbirds' and the 'Redbirds', and their RAAF allies. But as he so starkly puts it, the story of the B-57 in Vietnam leads to the rather bitter and inescapable conclusion that senior USAF officers of the period wanted to see the aircraft's contribution to the war effort officially ignored;

'The USAF "brass" loved us during the war. If they had a mission, we could do it. CAS, great. Stay on station for hours? We could do that. FACs loved us too, as nine 500 "pounders" and four 750 "pounders" on a B-57 was like a flight of four F-4s. Go north, but not in missile coverage, great. Fly great distances like 600 nautical miles into northern Laos on missions lasting three hours and fifty minutes without aerial refuelling (no capability, or need) and drop on road intersections? We could do that. Fly at night with flares? Okay, never done that before but we can do that. And we did. Fly with a C-130 "flare ship" at night? Okay, we can do that because the F-4s can't (too fast). Fly at night in Laos without flares on patrol? Okay, we can do that, but it was only a show of force (more like a show of sound overhead), but we can do that. Night alert? Okay. Fly escort with C-123s dropping Agent Orange? Okay. Every dirty mission, we could do it. And we *did* do it.

'But, after the fact, the USAF "brass" has tried to wipe us from the history books because of three incidents that marred the early days of our time in South Vietnam. The first of these were the deployment accidents in August 1964, which were certainly not our fault as we were sent in-theatre after being awake for 24 hours. We had no night formation flying experience. Secondly, the mortar attack which lost aircraft because there were no revetments, and finally the ramp blow-up due to World War 2 chemical time delay bombs. It was just too embarrassing to praise the Canberra units as this would have highlighted the USAF's chronic management problems of this period.'

B-57 and Canberra B 20 Losses in Southeast Asia 1964-71

Date	Variant, Serial (Unit)	Cause
4/8/64	B-57B 53-3884 (8th BS)	Landing accident
5/8/64	B-57B 53-3870 (8th BS)	Flying accident?
1/11/64	B-57B 52-1555 (8/13th BS)	Mortar attack
1/11/64	B-57B 53-3892 (8th BS)	Mortar attack
1/11/64	B-57B 53-3894 (8th BS)	Mortar attack
1/11/64	B-57B 53-3914 (8/13th BS)	Mortar attack
1/11/64	B-57B 53-3924 (13th BS)	Mortar attack
11/3/65	B-57B 53-3890 (8th BS)	Crashed on bombing run
7/4/65	B-57B 53-3880 (8th BS)	Hit by ground fire
16/5/65	B-57B 52-1568 (8/13th BS)	Airfield explosion
16/5/65	B-57B 53-3867 (8/13th BS)	Airfield explosion
16/5/65	B-57B 53-3871 (13th BS)	Airfield explosion
16/5/65	B-57B 53-3873 (8/13th BS)	Airfield explosion
16/5/65	B-57B 53-3893 (13th BS)	Airfield explosion
16/5/65	B-57B 53-3904 (13th BS)	Airfield explosion
16/5/65	B-57B 53-3913 (8/13th BS)	Airfield explosion
16/5/65	B-57B 53-3915 (8th BS)	Airfield explosion
16/5/65	B-57B 53-3930 (13th BS)	Airfield explosion
16/5/65	B-57B 53-3937 (8/13th BS)	Airfield explosion
8/6/65	B-57B 53-3882 (13th BS)	Hit by ground fire
19/6/65	B-57B 53-3910 (8th BS)	Enemy action?
29/6/65	B-57B 53-3895 (8th BS)	Hit by ground fire crashed landing
30/6/65	B-57B 52-1589 (8th BS)	Take-off crash
5/8/65	RB-57B 55-4243 (6250th CSG)	Hit by ground fire
6/8/65	B-57B 53-3919 (8/13th BS)	Hit by ground fire
6/9/65	B-57B 52-1544 (8/13th BS)	Engine fire
20/10/65	B-57B 53-3920 (8th BS)	Hit by ground fire
14/12/65	B-57B 52-1565 (8th BS)	Hit by ground fire
13/1/66	B-57B 53-3876 (13th BS)	Take-off crash
16/1/66	B-57B 53-3903 (13th BS)	Engine failure
10/2/66	B-57B 52-1575 (13th BS)	Unknown, lost on combat mission
21/2/66	B-57B 52-1523 (8th BS)	Hit by ground fire
7/4/66	B-57B 52-1530 (8th BS)	Hit by ground fire
14/4/66	B-57B 53-3925 (8th BS)	Mid-air collision with 53-3926
14/4/66	B-57B 53-3926 (8th BS)	Mid-air collision with 53-3925
17/4/66	B-57C 53-3833 (8th BS)	Hit by ground fire
13/6/66	B-57E 55-4268 (13th BS)	Hit by ground fire
19/9/66	B-57C 52-1541 (8th BS)	Hit by ground fire
6/10/66	B-57B 53-3888 (8th BS)	Hit by ground fire
8/10/66	B-57B 52-1512 (8th BS)	Hit by ground fire
8/12/66	B-57B 52-1590 (8th BS)	Hit by ground fire
21/1/67	B-57B 52-1557 (13th BS)	Hit by ground fire
22/4/67	B-57B 53-3859 (13th BS)	Hit by ground fire
3/6/67	B-57B 53-3862 (8th BS)	Unknown
8/6/67	B-57B 53-5908 (8th BS)	Hit by ground fire
19/8/67	B-57B 52-1550 (13th BS)	Hit by ground fire
10/9/67	B-57B 52-1510 (8th BS)	Hit by ground fire
25/3/68	B-57B 52-1592 (8th BS)	Hit by ground fire crashed landing
3/4/68	B-57B 52-1586 (8th BS)	Damaged by ground fire, later written off
23/9/68	B-57B 52-1498 (8th BS)	Hit by ground fire
3/10/68	B-57B 52-1570 (8th BS)	Crashed after engine failure
21/10/68	RB-57E 55-4264 (460th TRW)	Hit by ground fire
13/12/68	B-57E 55-4284 (8th TBS)	Mid-air collision with C-123K 'flare ship'
13/1/69	B-57B 52-1561 (8th BS)	Unknown, lost over Laos
22/2/69	B-57B 52-1532 (8th BS)	Hit by ground fire
15/3/69	B-57B 52-1567 (8th BS)	Crash-landed after hit by ground fire
27/3/69	B-57B 52-1508 (8th BS)	Hit by ground fire
3/11/70	Canberra B 20 A84-231 (No 2 Sqn)	Unknown
12/12/70	B-57G 53-3931 (13th BS)	Mid-air collision with O-2 FAC
14/3/71	Canberra B 20 A84-228 (No 2 Sqn)	Hit by SAM

COLOUR PLATES

1
RB-57E 55-4249 of Det 1 (*Patricia Lynn*)/6250th CSG, Tan Son Nhut AB, South Vietnam, December 1964
This aircraft was one of six B-57Es converted into reconnaissance platforms by General Dynamics under the top secret *Patricia Lynn* programme. The first two of these jets began operating from Tan Son Nhut in May 1963, and they were the last Canberras to leave Vietnam eight years later. The aircraft were fitted with new technology including infrared cameras and other elaborate sensors, and thus were kept under heavy guard when on the ground. This aeroplane is in the original natural metal finish, and it was later painted overall matt black. 55-4249 was retired to the Military Aircraft Storage and Disposition Center (MASDC) at Davis-Monthan AFB, Arizona, in May 1972.

2
B-57B 53-3888 of the 13th BS/405th TFW ADVON 1, Bien Hoa AB, South Vietnam, February 1965
On 19 February 1965 this aircraft, flown by the 13th BS CO Maj Howard F O'Neal and squadron navigator Maj Frank R Chandler, achieved the distinction of being the first US jet bomber to drop bombs in combat when it attacked VC targets near Bien Gia, 30 miles east of Saigon. The Canberra was carrying four 750-lb M117s of the old World War 2 box-fin variety under its wings, while in the bomb-bay were nine 500-lb general purpose bombs – the ordnance seen here under the port wing is a 500 'pounder'. The aircraft wears the early squadron markings for the 13th BS in Vietnam, consisting of a red nose cap, fuselage stripe and plane-in-squadron letter on the fin. On 6 October 1966 53-3888 fell victim to flak just north

of the DMZ near Kinh Mon, with pilot Capt G D Rippey being rescued by an HH-3E and navigator Capt L F Makowski captured.

3

B-57B 53-3929 of the 8th BS/405th TFW ADVON 1, Tan Son Nhut AB, South Vietnam, May 1965
After the Bien Hoa holocaust of 16 May 1965, yet more Canberras were immediately brought in to replace those lost in the devastating blast. One of those hastily sent to South Vietnam was 53-3929, whose only identifying marking at this early stage in its combat career was the yellow nose cap signifying that it belonged to the 8th BS. This jet soldiered on for almost four years in Vietnam before being modified into a B-57G and returning in 1970 to bomb the enemy some more. It was finally retired to MASDC in February 1974

4

B-57B 53-3925 of the 13th BS/405th TFW ADVON 1, Tan Son Nhut AB, South Vietnam, June 1965
This aircraft arrived at Clark AB, destined for Vietnam, on 11 May 1965. Just five days later came the flightline explosion that finally drove the units away from Bien Hoa and its dangerously crowded conditions. 53-3925 flew missions from Tan Son Nhut AB with the remaining aircraft until they moved to Da Nang some two months later. This aircraft is armed with 750-lb M117 general purpose bombs beneath its wings. 53-3925 was lost on 14 April 1966 when it collided with sister-aircraft 53-3926 during a practice formation flight over Da Nang. Both jets were assigned to the 8th BS, and all four crewmen survived the accident.

5

B-57B 52-1592 *Liz +3* of the 8th BS/6252nd TFW, Da Nang AB, South Vietnam, July 1965
The personal mount of 8th BS CO Lt Col Dan Farr and his navigator Lt Col 'Pappy' Boyington, this aircraft was kept buffed to a high sheen. It was one of the jets taken from ANG units to make good the losses suffered in the mortar attack on Bien Hoa AB in October 1964. The legend *Liz +3*, which is partially obscured by the port engine nacelle, referred to Farr's wife and his three children. This aircraft was shot down during a mission on 25 March 1968, pilot Capt R W Hopper and navigator Maj D L McHugo both being killed.

6

RB-57F 63-13503 of the 6091st TRS, Yokota AB, Japan, 1965
The RB-57F (later changed to WB-57F) was an outgrowth of the RB-57D reconnaissance programme. As the latter airframes reached the end of their useful lives, the RB-57F, with an even longer wing and greater intelligence-gathering capabilities, came into being at the General Dynamics plant in Fort Worth, Texas.

63-13503 was assigned to PACAF and used in the Far East to eavesdrop on Soviet activities. According to uncorroborated accounts, the aircraft was also used for electronic and photographic reconnaissance over Vietnam and Laos, although there are no official records available to confirm this. Originally built as RB-57D 53-3974, this jet was retired from USAF service by the 58th Weather Reconnaissance Squadron in 1974, after which it was transferred to NASA. Numbered '926', it is one of two WB-57Fs that still perform missions today from Ellington Field in Houston, Texas.

7

B-57B 52-1541 of the VNAF attached to the 8th and 13th BSs/6252nd TFW, Da Nang AB, South Vietnam, October 1965
As early as 1964 the USAF, at the request of the South Vietnamese government, began training a few experienced VNAF officers to fly the B-57 in combat. Although the programme lasted only a short time, Vietnamese pilots did fly some combat sorties. 52-1541 is shown here armed with 500-lb bombs for just such a mission against VC targets on 29 October 1965. The aircraft subsequently reverted to the USAF and was downed in combat on 19 September 1966, killing pilot Maj W L Gould and navigator Capt W S Davis.

8

B-57B 52-1532 of the VNAF attached to the 8th and 13th BSs/6252nd TFW, Da Nang AB, South Vietnam, October 1965
Often the VNAF B-57s were nothing more than jets taken from whichever USAF Canberra squadron happened to be at Da Nang at the time, and with their unit and national markings temporarily changed. Such was the case here with recently camouflaged 52-1532, repainted in VNAF colours for only a short time. The aeroplane carries four 750-lb M117 bombs on the underwing stations and nine 500-lb general purpose bombs internally. This was an early model B-57 fitted with four 0.50-cal machine guns in each wing. The aircraft was shot down on 22 February 1969, killing Lt Col D E Paxton and Maj C Macko of the 8th BS.

9

B-57B 53-3876 of the 13th BS/6252nd TFW, Da Nang AB, South Vietnam, November 1965
As the B-57s got better known to FACs and troops throughout the theatre, their old radio call signs gave way to simply 'Redbird' (for the 13th BS) and 'Yellowbird' (for the 8th BS), even after their colour markings were replaced with camouflage. Here, 53-3876 still wears the old 'NMF' with red trim. This aircraft was involved in a take-off accident on 12 January 1966 in which the bombs went off just as the crew had jumped from their aeroplane shortly after it had come to rest after bellying in. The blast killed

both the pilot, Maj E G Tollett, and his navigator, Capt L B Smith .

10

B-57B 53-3908 *Miss MiNuki* of the 8th BS/6252nd TFW, Da Nang AB, South Vietnam, January 1966

When the B-57s arrived in Vietnam in August 1964, they continued to sport 'NMF' adorned with their squadron colours – a yellow nose cap, diagonal fuselage stripe and plane-in-squadron letter on the fin for the 8th BS, and the same in red for the 13th BS. They also maintained the PACAF insignia on the fin and, very occasionally, nose art – this machine bore the name *Miss MiNuki*. 53-3908 was one of a handful of B-57s shot down during 1967 – the deadliest year of the Vietnam conflict for the Canberra in terms of jets lost in combat. It was downed during a night mission on 8 June, with both pilot, Capt E H Busch, and navigator, 1Lt P W Morrison, being killed.

11

RB-57E 55-4245 of Det 1/6250th CSG (*Patricia Lynn*), Tan Son Nhut AB, South Vietnam, November 1966

This aircraft was among the first Canberras to arrive in Vietnam. The small, highly-classified *Patricia Lynn* reconnaissance unit was transferred to Tan Son Nhut Airport in May 1963 and quickly began flying daytime photo-reconnaissance and night IR missions. It wears the matt black paint scheme that was applied to these aircraft in 1965 to better conceal them at night, as well as rare bat inspired nose art. 55-4245 and its three surviving stable mates were amongst the very last USAF tactical aircraft to leave Vietnam. Subsequently converted into a WB-57F, this aircraft was sent to MASDC in June 1972.

12

B-57B 52-1582 of the 8th BS/6252nd TFW, Da Nang AB, South Vietnam, March 1966

Following the airfield disaster at Bien Hoa AB in May 1965, the 8th and 13th BSs moved to Da Nang on a permanent basis, where it was believed they would be more secure. 52-1582 is shown here wearing the new four-colour South East Asian (SEA) camouflage scheme. The finned 750-lb napalm canisters, while not unusual armament for the Canberra at this time, were nowhere near as common as the 750-lb M117 bombs typically slung beneath the four underwing pylons. Converted into a B-57G in 1969, this aircraft was retired to MASDC in March 1974.

13

B-57B 53-3906 of the 8th BS/35th TFW, Da Nang AB, South Vietnam, April 1966

53-3906 was among the first group of B-57Bs deployed to Vietnam in August 1964. It survived almost five years of combat before being

modified into a B-57G in 1969. As with 52-1582 seen in the previous profile, this jet wears SEA camouflage over which the USAF's early individual aircraft identification system has been carefully applied to the fin. The jet also has light grey undersides, which were later painted black for the nocturnal DOOM Pussy missions up North. It carries four 750-lb finned napalm canisters under the wings, while internally the aircraft would have been loaded with general purpose bombs, often mixed with 260-lb fragmentation bombs. However, crews preferred the M35/36 incendiary cluster bomb units. This jet was also converted into a B-57G in 1969 (see profile 29).

14

B-57B 52-1499 of the 8th BS/35th TFW, Da Nang AB, South Vietnam, August 1966

Only the seventh B-57B off the production line, this aircraft was more than ten years old when it arrived in Vietnam. Like all early-model machines, 52-1499 was armed with four M3 0.50-cal machine guns in either wing, rather than two 20 mm weapons per wing as became standard for late-build B-57Bs. The aircraft is painted in the SEA camouflage scheme, with the early tail code style and light grey undersides. It is armed with four finned 750-lb napalm canisters on the wing pylons. Having survived its tour of Vietnam, 52-1499 was converted into a JB-57B target for high-altitude platforms and for the calibration of cameras. Later modified to serve as an EB-57B for use by Defense Systems Evaluation Squadrons, the aircraft was finally retired by the Vermont ANG's 158th Defense Systems Evaluation Group (DSEG) in 1982 and put on display in Hall 3 of the National Museum of the USAF at Wright-Patterson AFB, Ohio.

15

B-57B 52-1586 *CONG BUSTER* of the 8th BS/35th TFW, Phan Rang AB, South Vietnam, November 1966

52-1586, which has had its undersides sprayed matt black, has not yet had the new tail codes applied. The use of nose art among the Canberra squadrons reached its peak at Phan Rang, but for their Australian comrades down the flightline this practice was officially banned. 52-1586 is armed with M117s under the wings. These bombs, which were older warheads with modern tailfin units, finally took the place of the old box-fin 500- and 1000-lb bombs left over from World War 2 and Korea. This aircraft was written off in a forced landing at Phan Rang on 3 April 1968 after its crew had nursed the flak-damaged Canberra back to base from Laos.

16

B-57B 53-3877 *HELL'S ANGEL* of the 8th BS/35th TFW, Phan Rang AB, South Vietnam, June 1967

53-3877 was another aircraft to boast nose art

during the summer of 1967 at Phan Rang. The most popular means of applying artwork such as this was with coloured marker pens, rather than paint. This aircraft is carrying four M117 general purpose bombs on the wing hardpoints. It too survived five years of combat in Vietnam and was converted into a B-57G in 1969, prior to being retired to MASDC in March 1974.

17
Canberra B 20 A84-240 of No 2 Sqn RAAF, Phan Rang AB, South Vietnam, late summer 1968
The RAAF Canberra B 20 was an Australian-built version of the English Electric Canberra B 2. No 2 Sqn arrived in Vietnam in April 1967, where it operated alongside the two USAF B-57 units under the operational control of the 35th TFW. This jet bears the red lightning bolt that adorned the tails of all RAAF Canberras in Vietnam, which flew under the call-sign 'Magpie' – a reference to the native bird that graced the squadron crest. Of the 48 B 20s built for the RAAF, 17 of them saw action in Vietnam with No 2 Sqn. This particular machine was first delivered to the RAAF in April 1958 and issued to No 2 Sqn a short while later. It deployed to RAAF Butterworth, in Malaysia, when the unit was posted there that same year as part of the British Commonwealth Strategic Reserve in Southeast Asia, and it remained here until No 2 Sqn was transferred to Phan Rang nine years later. Note the jet's mission tally in the form of Day-Glo orange bombs painted aft of the cockpit. Such markings adorned most of the Canberras in South Vietnam, with each of the larger bomb symbols indicating 100 strikes and the smaller ones single missions. This aircraft, along with the remaining Canberras in RAAF service, was officially retired on 30 June 1982, and in August 1984 it was flown across the Tasman Sea to Royal New Zealand Air Force Base Wigram and placed on display in the RNZAF Museum at this location.

18
B-57B 53-3905 of the 8th BS/35th TFW, Phan Rang AB, South Vietnam, August 1968
By the time the aircraft were ensconced at the big new base at Phan Rang, they wore the ultimate Vietnam tail code style – two large letters that identified the squadron, followed by the serial number. The code for the 8th BS was PQ, while the 13th BS used PV, but after the latter squadron was deactivated on 15 January 1968 the 8th resprayed most of its jets with PV codes. 53-3905 was yet another of the original aircraft deployed to Vietnam in 1964 that survived to become a B-57G, although it was written off in a fatal crash on 16 December 1969 while being test flown by a Martin pilot. Conducting single engine tests with the jet prior to it being delivered back to the USAF, the aircraft crashed near Kentmore Park, in Maryland.

19
B-57C 53-3856 of the 4424th CCTS/15th TFW, MacDill AFB, Florida, December 1968
The B-57C was the dual-control trainer version of the B-model light bomber and night intruder, although like the latter it was fully combat capable. 53-3856 had served with the 8th BS at Clark AB prior to being transferred back to Florida to help train crews to fly the new B-57G as part of Project *Harvest Moon*. The aircraft was also used in the development of new tactics that were to be employed by the G-model in combat. This aircraft, fresh from the war zone, still bears the PACAF badge on its fin. 53-3856 was eventually retired to MASDC in December 1981.

20
B-57B 52-1567 of the 8th BS/35th TFW, Phan Rang AB, South Vietnam, March 1969
Originally sent over in May 1965 as part of the rapid deployment of ANG aircraft to make up for severe attrition at Bien Hoa, this B-57B soldiered on for almost four years of combat. 52-1567 was hit by groundfire while attacking VC positions in the A Shau Valley on 15 March 1969. The crew made it all the way back to Phan Rang before a dual engine flameout resulted in a crash landing, from which both men walked away.

21
B-57B 52-1551 of the 8th BS/35th TFW, Phan Rang AB, South Vietnam, October 1969
This jet is armed with four wing-mounted 750-lb M117 bombs for one of its last combat missions. Also an ex-ANG aircraft sent in January 1965 to replace those lost in the Bien Hoa mortar attack, 52-1551 became the last of the B-57 bombers to leave Vietnam on 15 October 1969. Its departure had been delayed because the aircraft required a last minute wing change. Subsequently converted into an RB-57B and then an EB-57B, the jet was retired by the Kansas ANG's 190th DSEG in 1978 after it had flown close to 7000 hours during its long USAF career. It is presently in storage at the National Air and Space Museum's Dulles facility.

22
B-57G 53-3877 of the 4424 CCTS/1st TFW, MacDill AFB, Florida, 1970
Of the 16 G-models built from B-57B airframes, 11 were deployed to Ubon RTAB and four were kept in Florida for training and further testing – as previously mentioned, one was lost during the new aircraft's development phase. This jet led the 'pampered' life of an expensive trainer, freshly washed and bearing a large 1st TFW insignia on its forward fuselage and the Tactical Air Command badge on its tail. 53-3877 has been armed with M117 750-lb bombs, which were not used by the B-57G in combat. The new LGBs were far too expensive to use as training rounds. This aircraft was sent to MASDC in February 1974

23

B-57G 52-1588 of the 13th BS/8th TFW, Ubon RTAB, Thailand, September 1970

52-1588 was originally on the strength of the 8th BS, flying from Da Nang and Phan Rang, before being withdrawn for conversion into a B-57G in 1969. One of the 11 aircraft sent into action with the 13th BS from Ubon in September 1970, the bomber survived its 20-month tour of action and was retired to MASDC in February 1974 following brief service with the Kansas ANG's 190th TBG.

24

B-57G 53-3929 of the 13th BS/8th TFW, Ubon RTAB, Thailand, October 1970

Yet another B-57B withdrawn from Vietnam and converted into a G-model Canberra in 1969, 53-3929 also returned to Southeast Asia in September 1970. When they became B-57Gs, these jets retained their original serial numbers, although this aircraft was fitted with the right wing of B-57E 55-4282 during the conversion – the latter was one of 12 converted from target tugs into bombers in 1965 and sent to Vietnam. 53-3929 was also retired to MASDC in February 1974.

25

Canberra B 20 A84-231 of No 2 Sqn RAAF, Phan Rang AB, South Vietnam, October 1970

The Canberra B 20 did not have underwing pylons or hardpoints for carrying stores, other than those for wingtip tanks. Since targets for the RAAF were all well within range without the need for drop tanks, they were replaced with purpose-made bomb racks. This modification was necessary due to the extensive use of long-bodied American 750-lb bombs in Vietnam, only four of which would fit into the B 20's bomb-bay. Two 500- or 750-lb bombs could be mounted on either wingtip to increase the bomb load. A84-231, seen here with US 500-lb bombs mounted, disappeared without a trace on the night of 3 November 1970 during a *Combat Sky Spot* mission over Quang Nam Province, southwest of Da Nang. The wreckage of the aircraft and the remains of its crew were not found until 2009.

26

B-57G 53-3889 of the 13th BS/8th TFW, Ubon RTAFB, Thailand, November 1970

After spending almost four years bombing Laos and North and South Vietnam, 53-3889 was also sent back to Martin to be modified into a B-57G. When the 13th BS returned to the theatre, it bombed targets along the Ho Chi Minh trail on most nights thanks to the G-models all-weather smart bomb capability. Indeed, the B-57G was the earliest aircraft to use the LGB on a regular basis operationally – in fact, on the wing stations they carried nothing else, and it was rare to see a 'clean' jet as depicted here. 53-3889 was also retired to MASDC in February 1974.

27

B-57G 53-3931 of the 13th BS/8th TFW, Ubon RTAB, Thailand, December 1970

This former B-57B was one of the first USAF Canberras deployed to Vietnam, arriving at Bien Hoa in September 1964 with the 8th BS. Like all B-57Gs, it carries first-generation 500-lb LGBs on its four underwing pylons. This aircraft had the unhappy distinction of being the only B-57G lost in combat when it collided with an O-2A FAC aircraft on the night of 12 December 1970. The Canberra crew survived but the FACs in the Cessna did not.

28

B-57G 52-1580 of the 13th BS/8th TFW, Ubon RTAB, Thailand, February 1971

The B-57G carried LGBs almost exclusively on its external pylons, while the aircraft's internal load was usually the spectacular and terrifying M35 or M36 incendiary cluster bomb unit. Here, the four bombs that could be carried are shown mounted on the rotary bomb-bay door, which is in the open position. The M35/36 carried hundreds of finned bomblets that spread white phosphorus and jellied naphtha over a large area just a few feet above the ground, consuming anything that would burn. 52-1580 was retired to MASDC in March 1974.

29

B-57G 53-3906 of the 13th BS/1st TFW, MacDill AFB, Florida, spring 1971

This former B-57B, after being upgraded into a G-model, was further modified as part of the *Pave Gat* test programme. The latter involved mounting a General Electric M61A1 Vulcan Gatling gun in the bomb-bay on a gimbal (which allowed the weapon to traverse a full 360 degrees) that was slaved to the aircraft's moving target tracking system. Although tested extensively, *Pave Gat* was not adopted. The moving target tracking system was one of the few major disappointments with the B-57G programme. The orange pod mounted under the wing of 52-3906 contains cameras to record the gun's movements. Never sent to Vietnam, this aircraft was retired to MASDC in February 1974.

30

B-57C 53-3840 of the 4424th CCTS/1st TFW, MacDill AFB, Florida, 1971

Many, if not most, of the rare dual-control B-57C models were recalled from Southeast Asia for use as trainers for the B-57G programme. With all but four of the G-models sent to the war, the B-57C was used as a stand-in for 13th TFS crews that were undertaking tactical training and proficiency flights prior to be sent into combat. Converted into an EB-57C following the retirement of the B-57Gs, this aircraft supported the USAF and ANG Defense Systems Evaluation Squadrons as a crew trainer until it too was retired to MASDC in December 1981.

INDEX

References to illustrations are shown in **bold**. Plates are shown with page and caption locators in brackets.